"One of the most powerful voices of his generation, Brandon Wolf tells a story of race, place, and the struggle for belonging that will drive you to tears and expand your capacity for hope, as well as your appreciation for the power of community. A true inspiration."

—Joy-Ann Reid, host of MSNBC's *The ReidOut*

"This book is both a necessary reckoning and a soft place to land. Brandon's story is a journey that challenges readers to not only find hope but also find the resolve necessary to take action. A must-read for anyone who wants to be filled with the spirit of progress."

—Frederick Joseph, *New York Times* bestselling author and award-winning activist

"*A Place for Us* is daring, raw—and necessary. The fight to end America's gun violence epidemic has long been grounded in the courage and tenacity of those most directly impacted. Brandon's survivor story will spur you to get up and fight for a better, safer tomorrow."

—Shannon Watts, founder, Moms Demand Action

"*A Place for Us* is a breathtakingly honest memoir that challenges all of us to rise above our darkest moments in order to courageously live as our most authentic selves."

—Igor Volsky, cofounder and executive director of Guns Down America

A PLACE FOR US

A PLACE FOR US

A Memoir

BRANDON J. WOLF

Little
a

Published by Little A, New York

www.apub.com

Amazon, the Amazon logo, and Little A are trademarks of Amazon.com, Inc., or
its affiliates.

ISBN-13: 9781542036467 (hardcover)
ISBN-13: 9781542036481 (paperback)
ISBN-13: 9781542036450 (digital)

Cover design by Rex Bonomelli
Cover images: ©Rex Bonomelli; ©OoddySmile Studio / Shutterstock

Printed in the United States of America
First edition

For Drew, who taught us to love with abandon

CONTENTS

AUTHOR'S NOTE

Perspective is a funny thing. It colors narratives and reshapes recollections. Crafting a memoir inherently means relying on a view of the world from one vantage point—one perspective. However, to the best of my ability, I wove these stories together honestly, taking care to capture them precisely as I remember them. In an effort to safeguard others' privacy, I have changed some names and distinguishing characteristics. Occasionally, events have been compressed and dialogue has been re-created. I hope, in the end, you'll find the journey as rewarding as I have.

PART 1:
THE BEFORE

CHAPTER 1

LOSING MYSELF

What I remember most vividly about the day Mom died is the smell: the deceptive, inviting warmth of fresh linens tainted by the sting of disinfectant. It's a smell I associate with death to this day, as if the stench of bleach alone transports me back to the stark white hallway of what was then known as Portland Adventist Medical Center. The smell hit the lining of my nose as my grandmother nudged me toward a tall hospital door with a thick window above the handle. Wires crisscrossed the glass, brutally juxtaposed against a clump of flowers on a table inside. I remember thinking that this must be what prison feels like, though I had never seen one. I turned the handle and nudged open the heavy door. A lump formed in my throat. Family members I hadn't seen in years were huddled around the bed, which was pushed up against a wall. Overhead fluorescents blazed, highlighting tearstained faces and accentuating dark circles under sleepy eyes. Monitors beeped softly in the background, eerie and hypnotic. On the wall, an oxygen machine whirred at its highest setting. And propped up by a stack of crisp white pillows was Mom.

My mother had always been tough. When I was still in pre-school, she took a job building manufactured homes. She was up long before the sun and pulled back into the driveway long after it had set. She was a single mother back then, my biological father having left when he learned she was pregnant. She could have been forgiven for giving up at any moment. For calling it quits. It would be years before she married the man I would come to call Dad, have two more kids with him, and finally be supported like she deserved. But she was determined to keep the lights on and food on the table. Somehow, in the face of grueling physical labor and the immense challenges facing countless single moms, she would nudge me awake each morning, wrap me in my favorite quilt, pour a coffee mug full of Cocoa Pebbles (because I insisted on dry cereal with a glass of milk on the side), drive me to my aunt's house, scoop me effortlessly out of the passenger seat, and *then* leave for work. At the end of each drawn-out day, she picked me up without revealing a hint of exhaustion and brought me home for dinner and a bedtime story.

But that day at the hospital, sinking into a heap of worn linens, Mom was a shell of herself. The toughness in her face had faded, her strong jaw hidden by cheeks swollen from infection. Gone was the tall, dazzling woman with long brown hair, pressing the toe of her knee-high leather boot against the accelerator of a cherry-red 1966 Mustang. Gone was our family's warmhearted matriarch, the fierce chef who demanded that we eat whatever she prepared while quietly making my enchiladas without onions. Gone was my protector, the ally who took me to a Spice Girls concert and bought me the last T-shirt on the shelf, who promised not to tell Dad when I performed living-room drag shows in it and a pair of her tallest heels. Gone was the commanding presence, the showstopping beauty. In her place lay a frail husk, a whisper of a once great woman, clinging to life.

Her chest heaved desperately. Her mask fogged with each strained breath, its elastic bands digging into her pale skin. Mom had first been diagnosed with cancer a few years earlier. After a series of misdiagnoses and inept doctors, an unsuspecting nurse discovered that her left lung had filled with fluid. It was panic at first. A rush to the emergency ward. A frantic call to Dad. Endless trips to specialists. Then we thought she had beaten it. We celebrated her remission, triumphantly hanging her go-to wigs from a post on the canopy bed. We rejoiced when a bone-marrow match was found. We told ourselves—I told myself—that this ray of light, the woman who had sacrificed so much to give me a shot in life, could never fall. Yet there I stood, my hip pressed against the foot of the hospital bed, watching her glimmer fade.

At Mom's request, each of her kids got a few private minutes to say goodbye. I crawled into bed next to her. My arm brushed hers, her skin burning, damp with fever. Through shallow gasps for air, she gave me instructions for how to go on without her.

"Take care of your sister. She needs you."

"Be patient with your father."

"Never forget how special you are."

The tears I had been holding in let loose, staining the thin blanket we shared. I wanted so badly to squeeze my eyes shut, then open them to find that it had all been a terrible nightmare. But my mother's pained face wasn't just a figment of my imagination. Her tortured grimace was real. Her hand, tightly grasping mine, was real. Goodbye was inescapable. Yet I wanted so badly to protect her, just like she had done so many times for me. Mom gave my fingers a knowing squeeze, summoned the strength for a grin, and shooed me off to lunch one last time.

It has taken me decades to face the life-altering isolation of losing my mom. Truthfully, it has taken until sitting down to write about it, and I'm still discovering that having my greatest advocate stolen from me has shaped, and continues to shape, my struggle to belong as a complex being in a world desperate to confine us into categories, checkboxes on an intake form. I didn't know how to articulate it then, but Mom was my first experience of a safe space. These days, the term *safe space* has been used as a cudgel against marginalized communities, a callous jab suggesting that those who need such spaces are not tough enough to handle the world as it is. But for people like me, people navigating the perilous crossroads of identity, safe spaces are shelters in a dangerous reality. They're the carefully crafted hideouts we carve for ourselves, sacred cubbyholes hidden from the harsh glare of a violent world that wants to devalue us. The spaces that were safe for my peers weren't safe for me. Science class wasn't safe when the bigots on the football team sat clustered in the back row of desks with spit wads. School hallways weren't safe when that one racist kid in his tattered hoodie skipped class to lurk around corners, waiting to slam my face into a locker. Church pews weren't safe when the pastor wanted to help me pray my gay away while the rest of the congregation turned a blind eye. Home wasn't always safe either, not after my family began grappling with grief, loss, and a son who didn't live or look like anyone else. When Mom died, I was too young to understand what sexual orientation and gender identity were, or that I'd ever need those terms to describe myself. All I knew was that I was different: a half-Black kid with white parents and a knack for musical theater. I didn't want to play basketball; I wanted to paint. I loved crisp white shoes and loathed playing in the mud. I didn't belong anywhere but in the arms of my mother. To her, I was perfect. With her, I was safe. And in an instant, that had gone. All at once, I was angry and terrified, left with only the memory of a few words muttered between desperate gasps for air.

Never forget how special you are.

~

You never forget your first. First kiss. First love. First heartache. They all burrow their way into your subconscious, destined to reshape how you see the world forever.

The first time I remember being called a nigger was sometime in my early teens. A friend named Jade and I were enjoying an afternoon in Wait Park, a local gathering spot when the weather allowed it. The sun was high in the sky, and no cloud obscured its warm rays. Sunny days always brought our sleepy, rural Oregon town to life and coaxed its natural beauty out of hiding. Birds flitted from tree to tree, occasionally chirping from carefully hidden nests. The smell of blossoms hung heavy in the air. Bees zipped from one colorful flower to the next, dousing themselves in dusty pollen. Kids laughed on the swing set, their untamed joy piercing the bustle of the summer afternoon.

Most of the time, I hated my little hometown. Rainy days outnumbered dry ones two to one, and months would crawl by without a sliver of sunlight peeking through the deep-gray cloud cover. The same faces roamed the halls at school, from the time you cracked open a kindergarten picture book until you scurried from one high school AP course to the next. Everyone knew everyone. And everyone's business. If you happened to get into trouble at school, your parents would know before you could kick off your shoes at home. The town seemed to run on autopilot, naively bouncing from one edition of *Groundhog Day* to the next.

The roar of an engine stopped me in my tracks, and I whipped my head around instinctively. Desperate to prove their masculinity, plenty of boys in town would roll around in jacked-up pickup trucks, oversize tires chewing up gravel driveways and black exhaust billowing from the tailpipes. Peaceful afternoons were routinely interrupted by the sudden growl of a cruising truck with a gaggle of rowdy teenagers piled into it. But this sounded more menacing. This sounded like a threat.

The tires squealed against the pavement, hurtling the pickup through the intersection and down the street in our direction. It was dirty and worn, the kind that would leave the trailer park on the edge of town at sunset to menace the neighborhoods of Mexican farmworkers, the kind of truck that was on the prowl for a fight. The front seats were occupied by two boys with familiar faces. I had seen them at school, wearing frayed sweatshirts and cracking jokes from the back row of the classroom. I took longer to tuck my notebook into my backpack at the end of classes with them, even if it meant being late to my next one, to let them barrel out the door and down the hall ahead of me. It was easier to be chastised for tardiness by a tired teacher than to have my head smashed into a locker by one of those two.

The truck slowed and pulled up next to us. I wanted to burst into a sprint, but I didn't want to leave Jade behind or give her the idea that I couldn't hold my own. I met the gaze of the boy in the driver's seat. He had a maniacal look on his face, his glassy eyes alight with a menacing rage, his voice gratingly high pitched.

"Fucking niggers!" he screeched, letting out a cackle and slamming his foot onto the gas pedal. The tires squealed loudly again, and the passenger howled with delight, repeating the driver's words in singsong fashion. The truck disappeared down the block; their howls faded into the cheerful chirps of birds. I suddenly realized how flushed my face was, a burning sensation pulsing across my cheeks, and the awareness made the embarrassment worse, so I looked down at the loosely knotted laces of my sneakers.

Jade and I carried on into the park, a pained silence between us. We haven't ever talked about that day, though it remains an ugly stain in my memory. I sometimes wonder if she remembers it as vividly as I do. Whether it was her first time too.

I don't know that I ever told Dad. I knew what he'd say in response: *Suck it up, Brandon. Those are just words. People say mean things all the time. Have thicker skin.*

At its core, his intent was pure. He wanted to harden his kids, to prepare us for the harsher realities we would inevitably face. But he was still a white man. He had survived an aneurysm in college, finding his footing again through backbreaking labor, climbing out of poverty with the sheer strength of his bare hands, holding our family together after Mom died—but there was no way he could understand *this*. To him, the word would have seemed cruel and heartless, but *harmless*, akin to the sharp language of any schoolyard bully trying to scrounge up lunch money. Hurtful, yes. But *dangerous*? Not quite.

For me, the word carried existential weight. It tore at the fiber of my being, threatening to come back, flaming cross in hand, to finish the job. It was a promise that if I dared to show my face in public, I would never be safe. It was designed to dehumanize and degrade me, to remind me of my place in the hierarchy. There was a targeted vitriol behind the driver's fiery eyes—his pupils dilated, his blood vessels inflamed—that Dad would never be able to fully understand.

~

Senior year of high school was going to be *my* time. I had toiled for years to assimilate into the community around me as I climbed each rung of the teenage social ladder. I wore the right overpriced polos, purchased with money earned at a part-time gig slinging lattes. I paraded my 4.0 GPA around like a badge of honor and added countless extracurriculars to earn my place in the pecking order. I doused myself in designer cologne and snuck out on the weekends to be seen at all the right house parties. Dad had remarried a few years earlier, so things at home felt slightly more stable too. This was my time to thrive.

Of the nearly two thousand kids in our school, only eleven of us were Black. And that meant that every hour of every day was a complicated fight for social survival. We learned to laugh off constant comparisons to [insert Black celebrity here] while learning exactly when the novelty of our color could help us stand out at just the right time. We managed to navigate incessant requests to touch our hair in the hallway and still make it to class on time. We were students but also survivors, strange faces in a sea of whiteness, donning whatever mask was necessary to keep us safe.

Life at home didn't make my journey any easier. My dad is white. His wife too. My late mother was white. My siblings are white. Classmates, teachers, neighbors—white. My biological father, the Black man who could have taught me how to move through the world in my mixed-race skin, abandoned me before even learning my name. And rather than push me to find that community elsewhere, with those who looked like me, that ubiquity drove me into isolation. I wasn't quite white enough for most spaces, and I wasn't quite Black enough for others. My family story was too complicated for a world reliant on binary labels and made-for-TV plotlines, and I lacked the language and curiosity to see value in each of my identities.

For years, I had been told that people *like me* don't succeed because they choose not to. I was inundated with racist propaganda meant to whitewash systemic failures—intentional barriers to homeownership, underinvestment in public education, the persistent legacy of slavery in our criminal justice system—and replace them with blame aimed at Black people: *They wear their pants too low. They don't speak correctly. They listen to violent music. They want government handouts.* My Blackness was made to feel like an obstacle—a disability—to be overcome. If I wanted a place in the world, those around me would say, I would have to prove that I deserved it. *If the world doesn't value you, it's because you're not working hard enough,* the most privileged among us would crow, their white, cisgender, heterosexual blinders shielding them from the ignorance in their own unsolicited advice. And I internalized all of it. If I could just show that I was *more* than others around me, I would be accepted. If I could just be exceptional *enough,* my caramel-hued skin would melt away, leaving nothing but the content of my character to be scrutinized. If I could divorce myself from my identity or slip on a new one like my ill-fitting polos, I'd be welcomed. If I could overcome what made me different, the world would finally see me.

Senior year was supposed to be when it all came together. But the miraculous assimilation of a kid fumbling his way through social no-man's-land was a mirage—and it vanished in the first weeks of the school year.

One morning I was perched at the kitchen table, scribbling notes for an exam, when the phone rang. I snatched it from its cradle on the wall and wedged it between a bony shoulder and my ear. After many nights spent whispering to secret boyfriends on the other line, I had become an expert at balancing the handset and twirling its long, tangled cord while my pen continued to glide over the pages of my notebook. Melanie's voice sliced through sharply, a ferocity in her tone that temporarily froze my hand.

"There's a white supremacist cell operating at school. I found their Myspace page."

For years, I've kept secret my paralyzing childhood fear of the Ku Klux Klan. I had countless nightmares of burning crosses, mutilated Black bodies hanging from withered tree branches, and veins bulging beneath white, sweaty hoods. We watched *The House of Dies Drear*, a 1980s movie adaptation of a YA mystery novel about a home haunted by the spirits of murdered slaves, in middle school history class, and I covered a mirror in the corner of my bedroom for years as a result. I woke up innumerable times in a panicked sweat, half expecting a Grand Wizard to be dragging me away by my ankles, only to coax myself back to sleep with the assurance that something like that couldn't happen here. Not in this day and age. And if it did, my valiant efforts to blend into the community around me would exempt me from their wrath.

But as Melanie's voice trembled with fury on the other line, I felt those familiar beads of sweat dotting my forehead. There was no jolting awake or coercing myself into falling asleep again—the threat was real.

The students pledging allegiance to white supremacy were a collage of faces I passed every day in the halls. They were football players and kids without an athletic bone in their frail bodies. The popular ones and the outcasts. A chunky wrestler with a persistently inflamed whitehead on his nose. A kid in a tattered gray hoodie trying desperately to hide the fact that food stamps were the only thing keeping his family from going hungry. At a glance, these kids had virtually nothing in common. They came from varied backgrounds and lived vastly different lives. No obvious threads bound them except their whiteness and their masculine rage, simmering and toxic. Their brewing hatred had been hiding in plain sight.

They had recently changed their profile pictures to proud poses in front of crisp Confederate flags, and they had buzzed their hair down to their shiny scalps. Their posts were chilling cascades of vitriol. One celebrated beating up a visiting basketball squad. Another wondered aloud which infamous band of white nationalists he might hitch his teenage wagon to. But one particular post got Melanie's attention, sending her blood pressure through the roof and prompting her frantic phone call to me. A hit list.

As I said, school was never a very safe place for me. I might have learned how to navigate the halls without getting stuffed in a trash can, but there was always an instinctive glance over my shoulder when I passed the boys' locker room and a flinch when "Faggot!" echoed from inside. To be the queer, mixed kid meant living in perpetual fear of a flying fist or a hurled slur. After so many years of unending fight-or-flight responses, carrying that fear felt as natural as the Western civilization textbook at the bottom of my backpack. But a hit list? The fine hairs on the back of my neck jolted to attention. The merry band of racists had, on a public forum, announced the names of those at school whom they believed would be better off dead. It read like a who's who of the traditionally excluded. The Black kids. The queer kids. The Jewish girl. All of us accused of not knowing our place on the bottom rung of the social hierarchy. I wanted to scream. And vomit. I had known that my carefully constructed persona as a "model minority" was tenuous (at best), but I earnestly believed that I had paid all the right dues to inoculate me from this kind of hatred.

Melanie hurriedly explained her plan to expose both our classmates and the school administrators who'd flippantly brushed her off with the old "boys will be boys" dismissal and shooed her out the door. She outlined her plot in masterful detail. Her voice brimmed with confidence as she described her intention to alert the media, share the posts with newsrooms, and highlight our leaders' inaction and the racist tensions simmering across town. Knowing that personal stories are the drivers of social change, she would invite the reporters to speak to those directly impacted. And together we would demand whatever shred of justice we could squeeze out from a community that would sooner sweep these ugly truths under a rug than allow them to tarnish its reputation.

It all sounded very Nancy Drewish on paper, but I was sleepless that night. Under a worn comforter, I rubbed my feet together to quell my anxiety. Maybe this covey of bigoted classmates was right. Maybe my campaign (and victory) for student body president had been too audacious. Maybe holding the microphone at every pep rally had been going too far. Maybe I got cocky. Careless. Perhaps people like me, those living in the creases of human identity, weren't meant to stand out. Maybe being brazenly exceptional didn't dictate my value to the world so much as my ability to perform exceptionally while keeping my mouth shut. I flipped the pillow over, quietly praying that the cool side would do the trick and quiet my mind. I felt paralyzingly alone. If Mom had still been around, I could have snuck into her room, curled up next to her, and told her how badly I wanted to understand my place in it all. I could have asked her if people like me are supposed to be seen and not heard. I could have told her how hard I'd tried to follow all the unspoken rules, while still coming up just short. Instead, I clutched a ratty bear she had given me and smelled its worn fur for any traces of her old perfume, hoping the scent would give me courage come morning. My eyelids drooped, weighed down by the day's stress. I let myself be hypnotized by the soft whir of a ceiling fan. *God, if you're real, please help tomorrow not suck.*

If hell has a physical manifestation, I'm convinced that it's a string of local news trucks parked menacingly outside your high school, the media eager to devour the dirty skeletons hiding in your closet. Melanie's plan worked better than we could have imagined. TV stations from across the city tripped over themselves to run the story. Reporters toed the invisible boundary across the street, watching students wander between classes, hungry for any controversial sound bite they could snatch up. Rural town's secret band of amateur Klansmen? That's prime-time content.

I waited until after first period to do my interviews. I should have skipped class as an extra *fuck you* to the school administrators who had shrugged this nightmare off, but being suspended in the first weeks of school sounded like a tough sell to my parents. My palms were slick with sweat as I stepped into the harsh glare of a fluorescent light. I had rehearsed my prepared remarks a dozen times, but my tongue still dried as the reporter thrust a microphone in my face. I can't remember now what I mumbled that morning, but I'm sure it was something diplomatic. An unequivocal rejection of bigotry in our school. A commitment to rooting it out and creating a space that was safe for everyone. A calm defiance and selfless deflection of the very real impacts of having my own name on that hit list. I know for certain it was an answer fit for a student body president who didn't dare acknowledge his crippling fear of the place he called home.

The rest of the day was a blur. I jetted from class to class, glancing around every corner for the gleam of a bald head. The reporters interviewed one of the racists a few hours later. Randy was a large, sweaty kid with a mop of greasy brown hair. I had seen him in the halls before, in a black trench coat, but I had never noticed the rage in his sunken eyes. He ranted about an "invasion" of Mexicans, the scourge of violent crime that follows Black people, and his unrelenting belief that the world should be rid of us all. It might have scared me half to death if it hadn't been so absurd. How do you grow up in a community and want nothing to do with the people who give its rich tapestry such vibrant color? How miserable is your existence when you see *other* before you see humanity? How stupid do you have to be to admit—on television—your role in creating a white supremacist cell at a public high school?

I don't know what I expected support or accountability to look like after the events of that day. In the pages of my diary, a fantastical place where Nate from history class was my secret lover, where the things that made me different also made me a hero, I imagined swift retribution for my classmates. A public shaming at city hall. An expulsion of their families from our neighborhoods. The sudden termination of the school's principal, a bumbling fool more intent on protecting his son's place atop the football food chain than on giving a damn about the rest of us. I imagined safety. Freedom. A place where people took a stand for kids like me, where those around me would lunge into action, resolved to do anything to protect us. But reality rarely resembled the faded pages of my journal.

Ours was a tightly regimented household back then. Strict curfew. Required church attendance. A ban on the Harry Potter books. And mandatory family dinners. I loathed that rule the most. After a grueling day of survival in the school halls, there was nothing I wanted to do less than sit on a hard wooden chair, stare at a mushy pile of microwaved canned asparagus, and recount the highlights of my day, tap-dancing around anything that might accidentally out me as gay. A firm knot grew in my throat that night, a physical acknowledgment that I would have to tell my dad what was happening at school. I stared down at the serving spoons, hoping to dissolve miraculously into my reflection. After a short prayer, everyone else went through the ceremonial recounting of the mundane details of their day: something about a project at work, a homework assignment, gossip from a neighbor down the street. I didn't catch much through the deafening thud of my own heartbeat in my ears.

When it came time for me to share, I cleared my throat a little more aggressively than usual, trying in vain to dislodge the anxiety that had taken up residence there. I took a sip from my glass and quietly imagined being washed away with its contents. Plunging into the depths of my own bowels sounded preferable to whatever was coming next. Without warning, the words spilled out. I fumbled through the details of a secret Myspace Klan, the pale cluster of peers whose names I had only just learned, and the fear I felt about going back to school. My voice trembled as I revealed my deep anguish to a circle of faces unlike my own. My hands shook as I admitted that I wasn't sure who to trust anymore. Breathless, I finally clamped my mouth shut, all the painful details of the past twenty-four hours splayed out like the remains of the meal in front of us. My dad furrowed his brow, pursed his lips, and stared at me from across the plates. He's a stoic man, well practiced at suffocating his emotions with a clenched jaw and a deep sigh. His piercing blue eyes had a furious glint as they lingered intensely on my face. After a long pause, he opened his mouth to speak.

"Maybe they have a point," he remarked flatly.

It takes a lot to shock me these days, and for that I credit my dad's propensity for responding to complicated situations by playing devil's advocate and pushing my buttons. I was used to these conversations with him. We had engaged in countless debates at the dinner table, a teenager arguing his position to a man longing for the intellectual companionship of his deceased wife and hardened by the cruel realities of being a single parent. My brother and sister, born after Mom and Dad got married, were mostly too young to find themselves in his crosshairs. They were still aimlessly scooting scraps of vegetables around on plastic plates in the years that Dad and I were embroiled in intense dinner-table feuds. They were used to tuning them out, and I was used to sparring. But this exchange stung because it was personal—not some abstract political conundrum or distant conflict divorced from the monotony of life in suburbia. My safety was on the line. And his reply signaled what I'd only ever whispered into the darkness after everyone had gone to bed: *I am on my own.* Surrounded by family, in my childhood home, I was painfully alone. I sat there, my face flush with humiliation, like a stranger who has suddenly realized that he's overstayed his welcome. I couldn't listen to the rest of his rationale. I pushed back from the table and excused myself, risking the consequences of abandoning family dinner in favor of hiding the tears suddenly pooling in my eyes. Where would I go? Who could I turn to? I shut my bedroom door and sank to the hardwood floor, tears spilling out. Most kids seek refuge at home and find safety in family. But I was deep behind enemy lines. And if I was going to survive, I would be forced to do so on my own.

I doubled down on my heavy workload as the school year dragged on. I figured that staying focused on getting out of school unscathed and setting myself up for college was the best strategy. Soggy winter gave way to slightly drier spring, the clouds finally parting just enough for the sun to peer through. I scored a lead role in the annual musical and came just short of qualifying for nationals in speech again. I nailed Western civ exams and talked the choir teacher into forgiving my shoddy attendance record. Things were shaping up nicely. Those in the white supremacist fringe had all been suspended or expelled. I was banking college credits, padding my résumé with extracurricular activities, and spending as little time as possible at home. Graduation was on the horizon. I just needed to coast my way there without making waves.

I dated a boy named Evan that year. If short-lived, it was my first notable relationship. I use that word loosely because dating another boy in a town stuck squarely in the 1950s doesn't look much like your standard tryst. We didn't get to drool all over each other in senior hall or get caught behind the bleachers, like our straight classmates. The handful of times we were brave enough to kiss were due to copious alcohol, a secret barn outside of town, and an intense game of spin the bottle. But we timidly held hands when no one was looking and barraged each other with scandalous text messages every night until one of us fell asleep or my prepaid data ran dry. He was cute. His freckled face was always rosy, his laugh infectious. It was oddly liberating to dip a toe in the waters of normalcy, which everyone around me took for granted. To have someone notice me in the halls and think about me after school. To put on my favorite underwear in the morning, knowing full well he wouldn't see them but feeling sexy for someone nonetheless. Up until that point, the other boys I had met went to different schools, were afraid to be seen cozying up with me, or "just weren't that into Black guys." If they noticed me, it was only long enough to ask me for my sandy-haired best friend's name. But with Evan, I felt secure. Happy. Loved. We silently understood that it wouldn't last forever. High school was coming to an end soon, and we'd go our separate ways shortly thereafter. But for an instant, we allowed ourselves to get lost in the warm refuge of companionship.

One morning Evan sprinted out the front door of his house, forgetting his cell phone on the nightstand. He'd probably spent a few too many minutes staring into the bathroom mirror, carefully sculpting his brown hair. This was long before the days of Touch ID and facial recognition software, so his mother just opened it and peered into her son's life. By the end of the school day, he was forbidden from seeing me again. He went back to eating lunch by himself and shuffling hurriedly from class to class, avoiding me. I played it off like it didn't faze me, but at night, in the quiet solitude of my bedroom, I'd stare at the tiny screen on my phone, waiting for a message. I couldn't tell if I missed *him* or missed who I'd learned to be while he was around.

I'd never really come out of the closet. In some ways, I assumed my queerness was obvious enough to go unstated. But I was also afraid to announce it. Coming out publicly would make it real. It would confirm the whispers and rumors I'd shrugged off for years. It would mean that the words I'd hidden in the pages of my journal weren't just a phase. Coming out would make me gay—out loud. Dating Evan accomplished all of that without me having to shout it from the rooftops. It just became real overnight. I had held hands with a boy. I had shown up to parties with a boy. I liked boys. And that was far easier to demonstrate with one of them ready to back me up.

Evan's mother was not alone in having a problem with this sudden revelation. News spread with signature small-town ferocity. A woman at church phoned the pastor for advice. Classmates whispered about me in the parking lot behind the tennis courts. Instantly, it seemed, everyone knew. And everyone had an opinion.

∼

Our big Diversity Week strategy had been hatched in response to the traumatic mess that kicked off the school year. The student body leadership team saw the best path forward as defiant and unafraid. More than one of us was Black. Most of us were more than a little queer. We were different. That's why our peers had elected us. And we were determined to use our visibility to push the community forward, not allow a noisy minority of aggrieved classmates to mute our voices. Selfishly, I wanted my legacy as the first student body president *like me* to be a school that I had left just a little gayer and browner than I had found it.

Our plan for the week was about as complex as any cooked up by a band of teenagers in the pre-Instagram age. A week of marketing. Fun themes for each day. All culminating in a Diversity Week assembly attended by the entire school. We would put the diversity of our school on display and celebrate all the things that made us unique. Sam had great handwriting, so we had tasked him with creating signage for the halls. "Make it good," we'd instructed. "We want everyone to feel represented."

Our little plot to bring the school together was bold, considering the year we'd had. There was no telling how people would respond to calls for unity, and we were bound to crash and burn if we didn't nail it from the start. But in our minds, if we could just get people to see past their standard cliques and stereotypes—to see one another—it would be a mission accomplished. Everything, down to the signage, needed to be flawless.

⁓

I wasn't there when the first poster was torn down, but I heard about it immediately. My phone buzzed furiously as the messages poured in. They ripped it down. It's been torn to shreds. Stay out of senior hall. My brisk footsteps quickened, and as I bounded around a corner, I nearly collided with Sam, his face flushed with anger. A small group of our classmates, most of whom had called me a "faggot" under their breaths so many times that I'd lost count, had been eating lunch against a concrete wall when one of our colorful signs sparked their ire. Its message seemed innocuous enough: *Love is love*. Adorned with two carefully illustrated hearts, it was among the smaller posters, an acknowledgment that we should draw as little attention to it as possible, but it was enough to invoke the ire of these angry teenagers, who gleefully ripped it from the wall and mashed it into the polished tiles with their muddy sneakers.

By the time Sam and I arrived on the scene, the last bell had rung. Everyone had stuffed their hamburger wrappers into overflowing trash cans, and all that remained were the torn and tattered remnants of Sam's work of art. If he was a nervous, chaotic creature, he was also intensely stubborn, often to a comical fault. He was notorious for digging in his heels, even when he was demonstrably wrong, until you relented and let him claim victory. More than once, he'd given me the weeks-long silent treatment over a disagreement about which music artist had the best new single or over a dispute about some boy we shared a crush on. Which meant that there was no way in hell he was letting this act of vandalism go. Sam's green eyes flashed, and his jaw clamped shut with fury as he picked up the battered poster board.

The next forty-eight hours played out in dramatic fashion. Sam repaired the original poster and affixed it to a more prominent wall near the front of the school, only to have a larger group of our peers tear it down and shred it to pieces. Their maniacal laughter echoed against the dull metal of the lockers as they took turns mangling the poster. Sam discovered what was left of it, crumpled in a corner, and went to work on a new one twice its size. Back and forth we went, Diversity Week spiraling from a celebration of our student body into a cold war over a rainbow-colored assertion that love is universal.

On the morning of Sam's frenzied recounting of the cafeteria scene, he unveiled our newest salvo in the ongoing battle. Inside the double doors of the lunchroom, he unfurled a banner, nearly twenty feet long, that made the message loud and clear: LOVE IS LOVE. He had garnished the bottom with crude stick-figure drawings of men holding hands and women in an embrace. It was glorious and petrifying all at once. This was bigger than sitting next to Evan after school, only brave enough to graze his hand with mine when no one was looking. It was somehow

20

scarier than the simmering silence at the dinner table after my parents discovered porn on the family computer. This manifesto—in bold block letters—was a declaration. Not just of our existence but of our inherent right to the same visibility afforded everyone else. My hands were trembling as our adviser unlocked the doors to the balcony and helped us secure the banner to the railing. The second level of the cafeteria had been closed off years ago, its tables and chairs covered in a thick layer of dust. Boxes of old supplies were crammed against the wall. Only a handful of teachers could access the space, which was an important part of our plan to protect the banner from harm. With a pound of masking tape and a quiet prayer, we struggled to secure it, giggling nervously as it swayed in the air blasts from a nearby vent. Sam beamed at his handiwork; the corners of his mouth turned upward in a defiant smirk. Lunch wasn't scheduled for several more hours, but I could feel a knot growing in my stomach already.

~

I always took the stairs to leadership class two at a time. Not because I had a particularly strong desire to be there but because I've always run late for everything. I had a habit of lingering just a smidge too long by my locker, then slinking into class a few minutes late. I slid into a desk under the whiteboard, still breathing heavily from the sprint up the stairwell. My best friend, Sam, midway through a story, didn't skip a beat. Despite having missed the beginning of the conversation, I tried to look deeply invested to avoid attracting attention from the teacher. We were in the throes of our biggest project to date, Diversity Week, and Sam was describing a situation that had unfolded in the cafeteria. He was a high-strung character, always speaking at a frantic clip and gesturing aggressively with his hands. His tone would climb into the rafters, just shy of a shriek, over even the most mundane of topics. Unless you spent lots of time with him, it was nearly impossible to differentiate between the truly urgent stories and those simply told with dramatic flair. Having spent the past few years attached to Sam's hip, I was an expert at deciphering between the two, and this sounded important.

"They built a tower of tables and chairs, climbed to the top, and tore it down!" he exclaimed, jutting the bony fingers of his right hand furiously into the air.

Our opponents, having amassed an indignant mob of fellow students, had stacked one lunchroom table on top of another, building a wobbly tower just tall enough to facilitate the capture of our big, gay, defiant display. Mere hours after we had proudly put it up, it lay torn and dirty on the ground. Another casualty. And the outrage was spreading through the halls like wildfire. Sam's stare burned into me as he impatiently awaited a reply.

"I think we need to chill for a day," I muttered.

Turns out, a day was all we had. The next morning, we were met by throngs of protesters at the front doors of school. They spilled off the concrete steps and onto the sidewalk, neck veins bulging as they shrieked homophobic slurs. What was once a siloed fire between factions of students had become a community-wide blaze of anger. Parents joined their teenagers under the cloudy morning sky and hurled hate at passersby. Adults and even children shook hastily made signs and furiously jabbed their fists into the air. They were angry about a bunch of queer kids with the audacity to love out loud. Angry about a bunch of Black kids with the courage to call out their ignorance. Angry about a community whose browner faces and busier intersections they no longer recognized. Angry at the realization that right under their noses, the world had made space for others. We were the target of their ire at that moment, but their rage had been brewing for a long time. I shielded my face with my backpack and pushed inside.

Over the years, I've seen the dangerous and manipulative nature of "bothsidesism," the nonsensical idea that to be unbiased you must give equal weight to opposing ideas, regardless of whether those ideas are worthy of equal weight. Think democracy and fascism. One gives self-determination to its citizens, while the other empowers a single leader to weaponize commerce, racism, and xenophobia. Equating them ignores the brutality of fascism and gives it a credibility it doesn't deserve. In the face of oppression and bigotry, twisting yourself into moral pretzels in order to appear neutral only leaves you with both feet squarely on the wrong side of history. Which is exactly what our principal chose to do that day, in spectacular fashion.

I shoved a stack of books into my messy locker and slammed the door. A printed flyer was taped to the outside: "It's Adam and Eve, not Adam and Steve." I ripped it down, crumpled it, and crammed it into my pocket. I knew the school like the back of my hand: the fastest route to the science building that bypassed crowded hallways, the stairwell that led straight to the coffee machine. I could follow these paths with my eyes closed. I had spent so many hours in those halls that they should have been like an extension of home. Yet I couldn't help but feel like I didn't belong. I was suddenly very aware of the stolen glances and hushed whispers belonging to kids who were eager to scurry away when I looked in their direction.

I'd barely settled into my desk during first period when the teacher told me to pack my things and go upstairs. The principal was waiting for me in an unused English classroom upstairs. We were just a handful of days removed from the poster saga, and I was grateful for the relative calm in the hallways. I took the long way, meandering through quiet corridors and past an empty courtyard. Our principal had never been much of an ally before, preferring to project an appearance of stability rather than ruffle any feathers in support of those of us who needed him. He and his family had been fixtures in our little town for generations, so there was his legacy to consider. He was, at the end of the day, most interested in preserving his standing in town. His primary goal would be to shut down the brewing insurrection. But what would be his endgame? Would he finally hear us? Take a stand? Demand not just order in his halls but a shred of common decency? I gently turned the handle of the classroom door, my heart pounding in my ears.

The principal was an intense man, short and stout with a tightly cropped goatee. He sat at one end of a row of desks, his thin lips pursed, eyes narrowed in a frustrated squint. He was clearly pissed. And judging by his tense shoulders and protruding jaw muscles, he didn't have much compassion for any of us. My friends—the Black kids, queer kids, Jewish girl, and our allies—sat in a row across from him, lined up like a panel of reality-show judges. A few had already been crying. Others sat in silence. I slid my bag off my shoulder and leaned against a desk.

"We're going to have a discussion with your classmates to resolve this," the principal explained. "We're coming to an agreement—*today*—and moving on."

It was anything but a discussion. A pack of our peers shuffled in, every one of them among those who had tormented us throughout our entire school careers: the kid who'd called me a faggot more times than I could count, the girl who giggled with me in leadership class and then whispered about me with her friends in the parking lot, those I could not wait to escape after graduation. The principal hadn't coordinated a good-faith conversation about how to make school safe for all of us. He'd engineered a standoff, the entire membership of the Fellowship of Christian Athletes versus the kids they saw as *less than*. The layout of the classroom was a physical embodiment of his naive assumption that both sides were equally valid, of his refusal to be anything more than a shepherd of the status quo. He saw us not as mistreated or discriminated against but as bothersome teenagers who might have it easier if we stopped trying so hard to be seen as human.

I've successfully repressed most of what happened in the hours that followed. Only small, loud snippets cut through.

Your posters are an affront to my religion.

One girl was sobbing.

Why can't you just do those things in private?

Another got up and walked out the door.

Don't you see you're going to hell?

A row of beady blue eyes, burning with the flames of indoctrination. Mouths frothing with hateful garbage absorbed at dinner tables and in church pews. Our principal did nothing. He sat wedged in a wobbly wooden desk designed for someone half his size, an overgrown child in over his head. He offered little more than a whimper as they ranted. A shrug. A heavy sigh. A nightmarish school year, the conclusion of a childhood spent desperately crying out for a place to belong, ended with exactly the kind of support I'd come to expect from powerful men: none.

CHAPTER 2

RUNNING AWAY

I pulled on my favorite pair of jeans, loaded the last of my things into the tightly packed trunk of the car, and shut the lid. I had imagined escaping home so many times that I never stopped to consider how anticlimactic the day would be. In the worn pages of my journal, my exit was a classic soap-opera scene. A dramatic, direct-to-camera monologue to air all my grievances. Tearful amends making from all who had made my life miserable for years. The great outdoors whizzing past as my hometown faded in the rearview mirror. All set to an angsty soundtrack by Alanis Morissette or Jewel. Everyone missed me in those fantasies. But reality was bland by comparison. I offered up a few hurried hugs at the screen door and got a reminder to "be careful" before sliding into the car next to Dad.

We hadn't talked much since the school year fell apart. The poster debacle was embarrassing, to be sure. It had left me feeling exposed among my peers, vulnerable amid the judgmental stares of other teenagers. But being gay at home was somehow worse. I was on the phone with a friend late one night when it all unraveled. The long cord of the kitchen phone could, when stretched carefully, reach just past the garage door without pulling the cradle off the wall. Like I'd done so many times before, I waited until everyone went to bed, slipped down the hall, punched numbers from memory onto the keypad, and carefully closed the door behind me to evade detection. I was beside myself. My voice was louder and shakier than usual. I rambled about everything transpiring at school: Evan was forbidden from seeing me. Things had gone from bad to worse, and I wasn't sure if I would make it to graduation. This was all news to my parents, eavesdropping intently on a handset upstairs. We tried to talk about it over the next few weeks, but every conversation ended with Dad's face flushed with frustration, deep and exasperated breaths escaping his flared nostrils. He was disappointed. Afraid. And the only way he knew how to express it was through hurtful jabs under his breath and silent rejection at the dinner table. I could tell he was still furious as we pulled out of the driveway. His cheek muscles tightened, his jaw clamped closed to prevent anything he'd regret from coming out.

Our pained attempts at small talk eventually faded into silence, the steady hum of the highway giving me cover to stay quiet and stare out the window. Most months in the Pacific Northwest are dreary and gray, tailor-made for corny vampire franchises, sipping cinnamon-dusted foam from the rim of a ceramic mug, and gazing at passersby from a shop window speckled with raindrops. I hated it. The soggy ends of cuffed jeans soaking through my ankle socks drove me crazy. I spent countless winters trudging through puddles to choir practice, longing to hang my rain jacket in the closet and dust off a worn pair of leather sandals. But if most months are dreary and gray, Pacific Northwest summers are nothing short of miraculous. The sky's gray hue gives way to a cloudless sapphire expanse. Fields, once dotted with dull green buds, burst into brilliant canvases of bright violets, mustard yellows, and scarlet reds. The air fills with a powerful array of smells: the sweetness of blackberry brambles and the sharp spice of Douglas fir trees. It's as if the entire world erupts into life, daring the onlooker to shed the weight of a long winter and step into the sun.

I snapped back to reality as we pulled into the parking lot outside a large brick dormitory.

"Don't say anything embarrassing," I told Dad as he popped the trunk and started unloading my things. I didn't know much about college, but I wasn't going to risk having my future in this new environment undermined by an awkward, incendiary outburst. I piled a stack of new bedding into my arms, sheets still smelling of plastic wrap, and walked through the open door. The dorm was old but charming. Its carpet was worn in places, a tale of the many feet that had trudged across it after long nights of studying and drinking with friends. The foyer gave way to a long, narrow hallway lined with doors, each appointed with a colorful piece of cardstock welcoming new residents. The building was abuzz with my new neighbors, hurriedly trekking their belongings inside so that they could shoo their parents away. I picked up the pace a little so that I could get Dad on the road and do some exploring.

After a few pleasant hellos, I opened the door labeled WOLF, scribbled in black Sharpie, and put the tower of sheets down on the bed. The room was tiny. I could sit comfortably on my own bed while resting my feet on the edge of the other. My desk, crammed into one corner, made for a tight squeeze. I took a mental note that the white brick walls would need some TLC if I was going to keep from going completely insane. But despite it leaving something to be desired, that tiny box was exhilarating. It was a new beginning. A place to reinvent myself. A secret hideaway. I exhaled for what felt like the first time in years.

Dad carried in a few other items, sat them down on the carpet, and looked at me with characteristic intensity. I think we both wanted to clear things up right there. I wanted to scream. And cry. And laugh. And hug him long enough to make up for all the embraces we'd skipped after fits of shouting at the kitchen table followed by hours of silence in the car. I wanted to apologize for not being able to see the world from his perspective and demand to know why he refused to see it from mine. I wanted to admit how unfair I'd been to him after Mom died and hear him acknowledge how unfair he'd been to me. I wanted a shred of the normalcy that other kids had been afforded, a sliver of humanity before he walked out the door and I stepped out into the world alone.

I wanted to tell him that, despite his refusal to accept me, I still loved him. And I wanted to hear him say he loved me back. In the strained silence, the weight of our complicated relationship hung heavy in the air. Dad sighed, leaned in for a tense embrace, said a hurried goodbye, and retreated through the doorway. In the quiet, I was alone.

When you step into a new world—where no one knows your name, your story, or the skeletons crammed haphazardly into your closet—there's a temptation to reinvent yourself. To scrub yourself clean of the dirty little secrets you're lugging around and put forward a polished, if slightly doctored, facade. I wasted no time in sloughing off my cowtown skin and rebranding myself for a new audience. I started by telling people that I grew up in Portland. A lie. Canby, a rural blip with a handful of stoplights and endless stretches of farmland, was a far cry from the bustling city north of us. But claiming to be from Portland invoked a particular image in the minds of others: vintage clothing stores, hip coffee shops, plumes of pot smoke, and an endless menu of tofu entrées. They envisioned a trendy, leftist woketopia where you can be whoever the hell you want and no one thinks twice. It also invoked a particular image of me: From money. Cultured. Progressive. *Worthy.*

A little white lie about where I grew up masked the truth about the nightmare I'd been through and sidelined classist questions about Drive Your Tractor to School Day. It inoculated me from having to explain the complex web that was my family, or why I didn't want to go home for Christmas. I didn't want to answer for my infamously racist classmates, sit through endless jokes about whether we had access to running water, or defend a community that had never lifted a finger to defend me. I wanted to start over. Turn the page. Blend in. Stash myself away in a new character.

But City Brandon didn't turn out to be a whole lot different than Country Brandon. I had wildly overestimated the change that would come from attending a state school just a few hours from home. In my mind, college campuses were bastions of diversity, rowdy melting pots where you got laid every night but still woke up in time for your

Bridging the Racial Divide course. And maybe that was the case for some, but it wasn't for me. My classmates looked eerily like those I had tossed graduation caps with just months before. Probably because that's exactly who ended up there with me. Parties were in dorm halls instead of wheat fields, but they still featured me as the token gay kid. The exceptions were the ones I attended with my hallmate Joel, during which we became a tandem act, drunkenly performing our favorite numbers from *Wicked* from atop the pair of twin beds to the delight of perplexed onlookers. I was hours from home, living on my own, and still sticking out like a sore thumb. *High School: The Sequel.* A collection of young people clawing at adulthood, armed with half-truths and over-size bottles of Jägermeister that we'd commandeered from a senior. The popular jock was now a fraternity pledge. The science-class nerd was now a biology major. This new world looked strikingly similar to the old one, albeit with a fresh coat of paint and an overpriced dining plan.

The early weeks of college were predictably about defining our new social hierarchy. That's a perilous and terrifying endeavor for those living at the intersection of identities, unable to rely on any one community for shelter. No single characteristic lifts us to the top of the food chain. You can't plop down in a cafeteria with people who look like you when you're not quite Black enough for one table and not quite white enough for the one next to it. And all of that is made more treacherous when you're too queer for any table at all. Those who were always at ease navigating the murky waters of social status slid into this new environment effortlessly, amassing friends and popularity without lifting a finger. The rest of us—those who had always worked twice as hard to find some place half as comfortable to belong—clawed for any spot we could find.

"Divide and conquer" has been a political strategy for ages, largely because it works. With our backs against the wall, we instinctively fall prey to the temptation of placing targets on others as an act of self-preservation. I wouldn't have admitted to it then, but that's exactly the strategy I employed as we jockeyed for social status in the early days of college. My roommate, Sean, was different from the rest of us. He was an unassuming guy. Standing several inches shorter than me, he had shoulders that slouched forward, making him appear dramatically smaller than he was. He spoke at a frantic, nervous pace and with a hushed tone, as if everything he had to say was simultaneously urgent and meant for only himself. He was remarkably intelligent, passionate about his education, and always on the edge of an anxiety attack. When he got lost in the heat of a rant about income inequality or climate change, he would grip a strand of sandy-brown hair between two fingers and twirl it furiously, eventually loosening a few strands that fell lifelessly to his desk. Sean struggled to fit in, constantly interjecting with the kind of comments that freeze a conversation and dissipate a crowd almost instantly. I could tell that, like me, he had struggled to find belonging throughout his childhood and wanted desperately to be part of a group. To this day, I regret never giving him the chance.

∼

It was one of Oregon's signature dark, dreary days as I strolled to class with my friends. Typically, carrying an umbrella was like donning a neon sign that said "I'm from California and can't hang," but the weather sucked, and I didn't want to be soggy throughout my next lecture. I clutched my umbrella tightly, futilely trying to protect my freshly relaxed hair from the cold rain. We meandered through campus, laughing at inside jokes from a weekend of binge drinking and lamenting our class workload. As we neared the student union, a voice cut through the patter of raindrops. It was shrill and panicky, amplified by some sort of microphone. It was also familiar. A peek around the corner confirmed my suspicions: it was Sean. Atop a makeshift platform, my roommate was shrieking into a megaphone that shook in his trembling hands. I couldn't make out his words through the sudden buzz of embarrassment in my ears, but I could guess that he was ranting about the university's sustainability plan or something equally obscure and nerdy. My friends giggled with glee, their judgment at his unhinged howling palpable, and shot me a glance. This was an unspoken test of the social ladder, a juncture at which I had to decide whether to endure ridicule all the way to calculus class or throw Sean under the bus and keep strolling. A few beads of sweat appeared above my brow.

"Weird Sean . . . ," I blurted, chuckling nervously. My friends guffawed, loudly hurling their own renditions of this new epithet in Sean's direction. His voice faltered and dipped in volume. He whirled around to identify us, his eyes locking with mine. They were pained and humiliated. I knew he expected better from me, the guy who had talked with him into the early hours of the morning about college, home, and the struggle to fit in. I knew he felt betrayed. I averted my gaze, staring down at the damp sneakers on my feet as we sauntered past, Sean's stare now blazing into the back of my head.

Without planning to, I had morphed into the kind of person I hated so intensely throughout high school. I was, in an instant, the classmate who had egged our cars during choir practice. A Myspace racist. The guy who called me a faggot every time I accidentally turned down 400 Hall. I had, without missing a beat, traded Sean's sense of self-worth for a fleeting taste of affirmation from a handful of hungover business administration majors.

That's the true pitfall of our desperate fight for belonging in the world. The system of delineating who's who is hardwired to devalue our unique identities, force us into boxes, inundate us with unrealistic images of what it takes to be worthy, and tempt us to shirk our very humanity by pushing others into the mud to avoid getting dirty ourselves, to keep us from realizing the collective strength of our communities. In tossing Sean aside, I burned a bridge we could have leveraged to improve campus life across the board. We would never build bonds around our mutual struggle to be good enough for our parents. We would never build trust through our shared grasp of what it feels like to be different. We would never form a relationship at all.

Sean withdrew from school a few months later. His mental health had spiraled, and his parents arrived one day, clearing his belongings in a flurry. I wish I'd gotten the chance to tell him how profoundly he reshaped my understanding of a person's value in the world. More than once, I found myself riddled with guilt about how I had treated him. I was always struggling to prove my worth to everyone around me, but he hadn't needed the affirmation of others. He just asserted his own value. I wish I'd been more honest with him about what life had been like back home for me—and how much we had in common. I wish I'd been able to apologize for using him as a punching bag instead of fighting harder for the both of us.

But I sat quietly at my desk, occasionally glancing at Sean's father packing the T-shirts into an empty laundry basket. Our eyes met briefly as he folded the bedsheets and mashed them into a black garbage bag. I imagined that Sean had told him about everything: the grueling class-work, the lonely library, and the evil roommate bent on ruining his college experience. I flashed a timid smile, my pathetic attempt at a silent apology. He met it with a steely glare, pursed lips, and an abrupt pivot on his heels. In an instant, Sean was gone, a casualty of this brutal, unforgiving social experiment conducted in a musty dorm, and I was alone with my thoughts in the low drone of the fluorescent bulb above the bed.

Floundering in the anonymity of campus life and the self-guided pace of higher education, I looked for community and acceptance wherever I could find it. I doused my insecurities in raspberry Bacardi. Passed out at frat parties trying to prove that I could hang with every-one else. I maxed out my credit cards, desperate to keep pace with the seemingly limitless resources of everyone else's parents, and I moved into an apartment I could hardly afford a few blocks from campus. My grades faltered as my social circle expanded. I wanted to be loved and appreciated, and it felt as if I only made progress when I was setting fire to my future, torching the values that had been instilled in me, and leaving a litter of damaged relationships in my wake.

Dating gave me intense anxiety in those days. It still does. And that's not terribly surprising when you consider that guys like me are assailed by a daily toxic cocktail of blond-haired, blue-eyed Instagram models, *no fats/no fems* dating-app declarations, and an "I'm just not into Black guys" refrain. Dating was (and is) prohibitive, akin to an Olympic sport reserved for those with superior social skills and beauty, as defined by ads and algorithms. On more than one occasion, I slid out of a passenger seat after what I thought was a night of intense chemistry only to find that my date had blocked me on Grindr before driving away. The whole endeavor was a social minefield that I avoided like the plague.

Sex was a different story. There is an intoxicating, if fleeting, sense of affirmation that comes with sex. In the heat of that passion, two bodies share an energy. The pressure to appear effortlessly interesting disappears. The complicated demands of human social interaction melt away. All that's left is carnal desire, a feeling of being wanted by another man. For young queer people who have found few other sources of love and acceptance, sex can be as addicting as any substance. I was particularly susceptible to its allure. In the absence of comprehensive sex ed, and with family members who were ignorant of anything beyond the postmarital missionary position, I was forced to learn about sex through AOL chat rooms and boys huddled by high school lockers. I learned about anatomy from hushed conversations perforated by childish giggles. I discovered sexting with men who were undoubtedly twice the age they claimed to be and looked nothing like the stock photos they circulated online.

I learned that, although it offered an endless reservoir of affirmation, sex was simultaneously seen as shameful. Especially when it came to gay men. The HIV/AIDS epidemic still loomed large, stigmatizing every act of intimacy in our community. Being together was dirty, an act meant to be kept in the shadows. And on more than one occasion, it was dangerous. But it felt good. Sex was an outlet. I could be beautiful to someone, if only for a moment. I didn't need abs or pale skin in the dark recesses of someone's bedroom. Sex was defiant. In the rush of passion, I could declare independence from the rejection of my family and the ridicule of my peers. But sex was also lonely. Just as quickly as the flames of a hookup ignited, they could flicker out, leaving me alone in the darkness, clawing for a towel to clean up the mess. Sex was a perilous game of escape roulette, leaving me seesawing between feelings of empowerment and emptiness.

I had a handful of invitations on New Year's Eve 2007. Back home for the holidays, I was staying with a friend and working early shifts at Starbucks to put a dent in my mounting credit-card debt. The easy, if mundane, option for the night was to join my high school classmates for a party a few miles from the store. We'd spent many a night sneaking shots from their parents' liquor cabinets, choking down flavored rum and seltzer and passing out on mismatched furniture. Option one was the safe, familiar bet. The other choice was a tad riskier. I had been casually texting with a guy named Ben for a few weeks, and he was aggressively pressing me to stop by his place for a small celebration. The persistence in his tone made me nervous. I had learned from a smattering of frat parties that pushy guys rarely have stomachs for rejection, and I didn't love the idea of meeting for the first time on his terms. But I also had no interest in sitting awkwardly at the end of a couch while girls in sequined tops made out with their boyfriends at the stroke of midnight. I wanted to have a New Year's kiss of my own, to live a little. And I felt the tempting pull of being the focus of someone's attention for the evening. I hesitantly pushed past the small knot in my gut and settled on the second option.

I'll be there, I texted.

Google Maps was only available on computers in those days, so finding a new location involved hastily printing a copy of the directions or scribbling them onto a nearby pad of paper. I grabbed a black pen and jotted down the steps on a piece of printer paper. Ben was already peppering my inbox with requests for my ETA, and my anxiety grew. Something didn't feel right, but I couldn't put my finger on it. Ben was unnerving me, his messages coming in faster than I could respond. But I shrugged it off. I'd already pressed a crisp cotton shirt for the evening.

I folded the paper, grabbed my backpack, and slipped quietly out the front door. My sweet cologne hung thick in the car, giving me a headache, so I cracked the window, inviting a cold blast of winter air. This was a terrible idea. Waltzing into a stranger's home, downing cheap champagne, and hoping for the best would have made my parents' heads explode. And maybe that was part of the thrill. To live carelessly, to toss myself into the arms of someone I might never see again, was also to stubbornly declare myself worthy of the kind of affection I had been denied. I pressed my foot harder on the pedal, the growl of the engine drowning my racing mind.

I pulled into Ben's neighborhood and started this careful dance, winding slowly down the street to avoid missing my turn. The parking lot of his apartment complex was dimly lit by orange streetlights wan after years of neglect. I inched into a spot whose VISITOR label had long since cracked and faded away. *Last chance,* I thought. *You can still turn around.* I opened the car door, slung the strap of my bag over one shoulder, and stepped out into the night.

Ben's apartment was a dingy bachelor pad, its carpet dirty and worn, a faint smell of mildew hanging in the air. In the living room, a couch with sagging cushions sat across from a small television perched atop a cheap plywood stand. His friends, shouting chaotically, knelt around a sticky coffee table littered with playing cards and red plastic cups. I stepped past the threshold, grinding their conversation to a halt. Their heads turned slowly, scanning me up and down, a judgmental but customary greeting among gay men. I could immediately tell which of them was interested in Ben, as his eyes narrowed more than the others' and locked briefly with mine. I slid onto one end of the couch and fumbled with my key chain.

"You want a shot?" someone slurred loudly, shattering the tension. I accepted, relieved. Two ounces of cut-rate vodka burned their way down my throat.

When Ben stepped into the bathroom, his friend grabbed my forearm aggressively, pulling his flushed face close to mine. The smell of liquor on his hot breath stung my nose.

"Be careful around Ben," he slurred. "He's not the most trustworthy."

I was officially unsettled. Red flags were everywhere: the aggressive text demands, the jealous love interest burning holes through the back of my head, Ben's hand gripping my waist just a little too tightly, despite my resistance, and Ben watching me like an entrée while pouring me glass after glass of champagne. This new warning confirmed that whatever defiant act of indulgence I had planned for the evening was a mistake. I needed to plot an exit.

I took note of my bag sitting a few steps from the couch, knowing I'd need to grab it discreetly. I tried formulating a plan, but my head was swimming from the alcohol. I had no idea what I would do once I climbed behind the wheel of my car, but I didn't care. Anything to get me out, to somewhere I could lock the door. If I could just sit for a few minutes, my head would clear, and I could execute my escape. I stumbled to my feet and careened toward the couch. My head was spinning, my fingers tingling. I collapsed onto a stained cushion, the ceiling whirling above me. I could get out if I could just . . . Everything went dark.

I snapped back to reality in the shadows of Ben's bedroom. His sweaty hands gripped my shoulders. He was grunting like some prehistoric animal devouring its prey. Every muscle in my body clenched while he forced himself inside me again and again. The smell of liquor on his breath mixed with the pounding in my own head and made me want to vomit. I don't know if I begged him to stop out loud or if my screams remained trapped behind my grinding teeth. Every inch of me felt like it was exploding, and my skin tingled numbly. My legs quivered, and I could feel a dampness underneath my knees. A panicked survey with the pads of my fingers revealed a layer of liquid on the sheets—blood, and lots of it. Tears streaked down my face before plunging to the bedding. I looked around frantically in a futile attempt to find help. In an act of self-preservation, I retreated into the recesses of my mind, images of my childhood flashing between spurts of reality in a kaleidoscope of dissociation. Wind rushing past my ears on a secret bike ride to the doughnut shop with my cousin. Ben's sweaty face lurching over me. The smell of freshly baked apple pie on my grandmother's back porch. Ben's long, dirty fingernails clawing into the soft skin covering my shoulder blades. The feeling of soft grass between my toes on the soccer field. Stinging pain radiating up and down my legs. Everything went dark again.

When I regained consciousness, Ben was snoring, one hairy arm draped across me like a seat belt. The blankets were tossed into a heap, pools of my blood dried onto the sheets. I was disoriented but more coherent than at any point since arriving. I wriggled a little, gauging the depth of his slumber. His snoring continued unabated, so I slid free of his arm, inching toward the edge of the bed. I realized I was holding my breath, and the lack of oxygen intensified a shooting pain in both temples. My toes grazed the carpet, and I let out a silent sigh of relief. Freedom was the sliver of light peeking around the door, which had been left ajar. I hastily pulled on my clothes, ignoring throbbing pain from several parts of my body, and crept through the door.

It wasn't until I had tiptoed through the kitchen and closed the front door of the apartment that I finally wept. I was embarrassed. Infuriated. Heartbroken. Violated. I felt responsible for putting myself in such an unfathomable position and ashamed at having been lured into danger by the temptation of momentary satisfaction. I felt like I had gotten what I deserved: punishment for being a member of the shameful underbelly of society. The rabid mob scaling a tower of lunch tables had been right. Dad, his furious gaze fixed on a sad heap of mashed potatoes, had been right. This is what happens to people *like me*. I slunk into the driver's seat of my car and slapped both sides of my face to try to sober up. My hands were shaking so violently that I couldn't get the key into the ignition. I took a few deep breaths and wiped away the tears. If anyone found out about this, I would be done.

People would whisper under their breaths about the guy who's easy. Any social status I had accrued would be torched. I flipped down the visor, peered into my bloodshot eyes in the mirror, and made a quiet vow: *Bury this.*

And I kept that vow—until now. This is the first time I've ever recounted what happened that night. I tried to press on, covering the deep sense of shame foisted upon me by a man whose last name I never learned. I went to work that day, plastered on a pleasant expression, and busied myself with a long line of lattes. The coffee business booms during the holidays, so there was little downtime. Keeping track of milk preferences, topping choices, and the familiar faces of regular customers kept my mind from wandering back to the horrors of the night before.

I drove the usual streets home. Tucked into familiar sheets. And when winter break ended, I loaded my bags into the trunk of the car and headed back to my apartment off campus. To the average observer, everything was fine. I went to parties. Drank from wine bottles smuggled into the apartment in my roommate's purse. Dozed off in lecture halls. Begged for leftover food at the end of my shifts. But to anyone who looked close enough, the signs were there. I had run out of things to live for. I flinched at human contact. Looked away when passing a mirror. Cried myself to sleep each night. Iced the heavy bags under my eyes the next morning.

I became angrier, my temper shorter. One night, I had a date lined up with a boy who was light-years out of my league. I can't remember his name or where we were supposed to go, but in my shortsightedness, I was sure that this date was when I would finally find my groove. He texted to cancel a few hours before we had planned to meet: I realized I'm just not that into Black guys—sorry. Though I'd heard those words countless times, my anger flared, and my cheeks flushed with fury. Without thinking, I picked up a tattered sneaker and hurled it so hard that it shattered the mirror propped in the corner, its fractured shards a fitting metaphor for my life.

My grades sputtered, plunging me further into despair. A letter came, informing me that I was being placed on academic probation. My ability to achieve had always defined me. Others had athletic talent, charm, or good looks, but I was just determined to be good at anything I set my mind to. When the world counted me out—too Black, too white, too skinny, too gay—I responded by outworking everyone around me. Now that superpower was evaporating right in front of me. How the hell was I going to amount to anything more than what the naysayers had predicted? I needed a lifeline. A sign.

∿

I worked for Starbucks for many years and in a number of cities, and not one was like the campus store at the University of Oregon in the 2000s. Most people associate coffee shops with their senses: the sound of beans grinding alongside a playlist of plodding, identical-sounding folk songs, the taste of creamy milk foam swirling with rich espresso, the smell of freshly ground coffee and sweet pastries. Our store threw all that out the window. We shared the lobby with a sandwich shop, which meant that the warm smells of nutmeg and cinnamon were replaced with the stinging scent of red onions and mustard. It was also constantly busy and loud. The line ebbed and flowed in tandem with class schedules amid the unending din of students cramming for exams and gossiping about roommates. The job always demanded a grueling pace. Get stuck on the espresso bar for a shift and your back and fingers would ache from the relentless, repetitive motion. Add the impatient demands of hungover college students shouting over the screams of steaming milk, and it was an utterly exhausting place to work.

The night before my shift, I'd been up late studying for an international relations exam. Though most of the courses I took were painfully boring to me, I found global politics fascinating. I could pore effortlessly over texts on Middle East relations until the sun peeked over the horizon, but getting up for work afterward was a challenge. Under the

41

hood of my dingy white sweatshirt that morning, I seized every opportunity to lean against the counter. I had gotten so caught up in studying that I had forgotten to do laundry, so my shirt smelled of onions, and my apron had a thin layer of spoiled whipping cream on the front. My stomach growled, a steady reminder of my overdrawn bank account and the kitchen cabinets that would remain empty until payday. My supervisor's voice cut through the whir of the coffee grinder and Sia's nasal melody blaring from the speakers.

"Brandon, take your fifteen," she said.

Thank God. I rummaged through the expired food bin in the back of the refrigerator for something to quell my rumbling belly. A bagel in plastic wrap was firm but soft enough to eat, so I stuffed it into the pocket of my apron and collapsed into a chair. Alone and exhausted, my mind wandered while I nibbled. The refrigerator at home was empty, and I wouldn't get a paycheck for days. Rent was coming due. What to do about the electric bill? How did anyone succeed in this environment without begging their parents for money? Recovering from academic probation required that I do well as a full-time student. I was totally screwed.

I suddenly became aware of my supervisor, Karyn, towering menacingly over me. She was tall and intimidating by nature, and I sat upright unconsciously. I hastily checked the time on my phone, worried that I had daydreamed and overextended my break.

"I saw this and thought of you," she said with a smirk, thrusting a school newspaper into my hand. Karyn and I had formed a close bond over the last couple of years. She was among the few people I'd met whose authenticity was contagious. I couldn't explain why, but she made me feel safe. We frequently made silly jokes and talked about music, so I half expected to find some funny headline, nonsensical cartoon, or concert ad in the newspaper, but in the top right corner was a tiny square with the Disney logo and bold black print: HELP WANTED. AUDITION SOON. Karyn's smirk turned into a toothy one.

Life is a collection of choices, a series of decisions made along a timeline that, in its totality, forms our stories. Some choices are inherently small: what to eat for dinner, which pair of socks to wear. Some are naturally more defining: the decision to go to college, to accept a marriage proposal. And still others feel insignificant at the outset but come to shift one's trajectory entirely. Groggily peering at the damp newspaper, I made one of those choices: to imagine something different. The unassuming want ad challenged every perception I had about what value I could offer the world. I'd been taught that success was part of a linear progression. You work hard in high school, study something "real" in college, walk the stage at graduation, and get a desk job in some midsize city with affordable home prices. You build a white picket fence to keep two kids and a dog from getting out. You fit in. I had spent years internalizing the idea that in order to be someone the world isn't ready for, you have to be exactly what you're told. Yet peering back at me from the page was a different path, a playful rejection of the rules that had tightly guarded all my prior decisions.

HELP WANTED. AUDITION SOON. Where others might see dropping out, I imagined moving on. Where some might see uncertainty, I imagined possibility. With a single choice, I could buck the path that others had imagined for me, pick up the pieces, and be free. My cell phone alarm buzzed, marking the end of my break. I folded the paper, peered up at Karyn, whose face was twinkling with excitement, and smiled.

A sign.

CHAPTER 3

DISCOVERY

"Ten minutes to set, Tigger."

I looked up from my book as the character attendant stepped outside and closed the door behind her. I folded one corner of the page, closed it, and shuffled over to my costume on the opposite wall. I had imagined a lot of things about working at Disney—myself on the set of *High School Musical*, basketball in one hand and multicolored pom-pom in the other; bright lights and big stages; crowds cheering my name as I belted out the highest note in my range. I had no basis for these assumptions, but I had imagined something as glamorous as the made-for-TV movies on the Disney Channel. I had not imagined wearing a sweaty rug for hours a day, sweltering in the sun as spoiled children pounded my oversize helmet and tugged my arms. I pulled my cold, wet black tights back on and slipped into my furry orange costume.

So much about starting over in Orlando was different, disorienting. The air hung heavier than at home, a deep humidity slowing the pace of everything to a Southern crawl. The food was spicier and fried into crispy oblivion. The distant mountains and endless winter drizzle of home were replaced by long, flat stretches of swampland and torrential downpours on the hottest days of the year. It was overwhelming and frustrating at times. I had left my car at home and now relied on public transportation. The unreliability of the bus was often painful, my final sprint to the time clock after another bus delay leaving me gasping for air. The pay was miserable, and I could afford little more than cases of ramen noodles and an occasional box of Pop-Tarts. More than once, I debated repacking my two worn suitcases and booking the first flight back to the West Coast, ducking out without so much as a farewell to anyone.

But for every difficult adjustment, there were more exhilarating ones. Late-night walks to a nearby lake to stare up at the stars and listen to the alligators grunt. Dipping toes into the Atlantic Ocean. Savoring fresh-caught seafood at a beachside bar. Riding roller coasters again and again, until the world wouldn't stop spinning. Learning Korean from one roommate while teaching French to another. This new place was like an uncorked fire hydrant of new experiences, threatening to either drown me in culture shock or leave me free of thirst forever.

I shared an apartment with three people, each from a different part of the country. The living room was sparsely furnished with a chaotic mismatch of seats, tables, and lamps. We had dug the sofa out of a dumpster near the front of the complex and hid its stains by flipping the cushions over. A small television sat atop a rickety table that we'd put together after more than a few cocktails. One frayed end of an unused cable jutted from a hole in the wall. The kitchen was dated and worn, one overhead bulb casting an intense spotlight on the peeling countertops and grungy linoleum. Late at night, a stray cockroach sometimes scurried across the floor, surveying corners for overlooked crumbs. It might have bothered us, but we didn't have the money or energy to complain. Sure, it was a grimy hole-in-the-wall. But it was *our* grimy hole-in-the-wall.

Despite working multiple jobs, our paychecks were woefully inadequate. We often went for days with empty cupboards and a barren refrigerator. I invented new recipes with saltine crackers. My roommates stretched their food stamps. We kept an emergency box of pasta stashed above the stove, drank cheap liquor by the liter, and sustained ourselves with macaroni and cheese. A thin haze of cannabis smoke always drifted through the apartment, a vaporous sign of how my roommates were attempting to cope with all of the above.

On some days, it was the worst of times. I stopped answering my phone when the only callers were debt collectors threatening to garnish my wages. I battled through a dangerous respiratory infection, armed with only a handful of expired Motrin that I dug out of a bathroom drawer. A visit to urgent care cost several times what was left in my checking account. But on most days, I was living a personal revolution. The physical demands of my job shaved off what remained of my baby weight, revealing a body I didn't recognize in the mirror. I would stand naked in front of it after a shower and admire the faintly defined abs. I joined in break-room conversations with other queer people, gossiping about late-night trysts and giggling about the latest pop-culture headlines, a far cry from the high school jury of my peers condemning me to fiery hell for daring to hold hands with a boy. I listened to Lady Gaga at maximum volume without wondering whether the neighbors could hear. I had sex with boys without paralyzing self-doubt. I woke up late on weekends, took long daily showers, and spent evenings exploring hidden corners of Orlando's theme parks. The freedom of a new world was intoxicating.

For every day I spent trying to tame my growling stomach, there were four others in which I devoured every wild new adventure the world threw at me. I had imagined that college was where young people went to discover themselves, make mistakes, and defy all the guidance their parents had given them. For some, that's true, but for me, the chains came off in the City Beautiful.

~

I scooted closer to the tall mirror stretching up from the gymnasium floor. Mirror spots in the break room were prime real estate, typically reserved for the prettiest performers, who donned blond princess wigs, and their favorite dancer boys. The rest of us were relegated to a space near the exercise balls, forced to peer into handheld mirrors or squeeze in behind someone's oversize ball gown.

I arrived early that afternoon, having scarfed down a pile of pasta from a cafeteria tray and hitched a golf-cart ride across the park. After staking a claim on a coveted sliver of reflective glass in the corner, I was met with glares and irritated whispers. I had worked hard to put the days of a furry costume and endless photos with shrieking children behind me. Though I had no formal dance training (and arguably not much skill), I knew that I wanted to be cast in a parade. It meant a fifty-cent pay increase, the difference between keeping the kitchen cupboards stocked or not, as well as reliable hours, long breaks, and a perceived social status upgrade. Never mind that everyone was practically starving and forced to dance despite persistent injuries. Being cast in a parade was as close to prestige as it got at a profit-hungry theme park employing hundreds of college-age dreamers. So I toiled at auditions and begged the casting directors until I finally got my chance. And now I was positioned squarely in front of *the mirror*.

A steady stream of performers flowed through the doors. Exaggerated cartoon costumes were flung onto posts, and workers settled into their usual cliques. I turned briefly and waved to a few friends but averted eye contact when they called for me to sit with them. There was no way I was giving up that ideal slice of real estate. They called to me again, but I pretended not to hear, cramming a headphone deeper into my ear.

Boys were explicitly told not to wear makeup during parades. The company had a litany of excuses for the gendered distinction: *It will ruin the costume. It doesn't fit the look. We don't want you using up expensive products.* But no matter what varnish was slapped on the reasoning, we all knew the truth. The company was worried that we would look *too gay*. Our powdered noses and contoured brows would shatter the illusion that the company was feeding to families, its customers, that dance partners in parades were all joyful heterosexual couples. We were expected to play our parts, despite our bejeweled vests and bedazzled suit pants. A little foundation felt like an act of homosexual resistance, so I took advantage of my segment of mirror and blended a bit of the tan liquid into my skin.

As I dabbed my face with an orange sponge, I got the sense that I was being watched. I glanced over my shoulder to see that a familiar group of boys had sidled up next to me to watch as I readied myself for the show. They were among the most recognizable Black boys in the department, having learned nearly every show across the array of theme parks under the Disney brand. They were wildly talented and stunningly beautiful, their ebony skin free of imperfections and always glistening perfectly in the summer sun. Theirs was a prestige well earned. And they almost always kept to themselves, loath to make small talk with those outside their selective circle. I chuckled sheepishly and went back to blotting my face. They remained fixated on me, watching with intense curiosity. I busied myself, hoping they would go away, until one cleared his throat.

"Why is your lineup like that?" he asked, pointedly.

I blinked. I had no idea what he was talking about, though I assumed he was referring to the way I had applied my makeup. Admittedly, I was about as savvy with a beauty blender as I was with complicated choreography, so I wasn't surprised that someone finally noticed my amateur attempts at applying foundation. I chuckled nervously. "I know, I'm a little clumsy with it," I said, brushing my cheek with a pair of fingers, as if to acknowledge where I'd gone astray.

The boys giggled aggressively.

"No, your *lineup*," he said again, turning to the mirror and pointing to my temple. I looked back quizzically. Nothing about my temples had ever seemed odd before. What had I been missing? "Your hairline." He was growing irritated. "It's rounded when it should be squared off. Only girls have hairlines like that."

I looked harder into the mirror, aware of the shape of my hairline for the first time. How had I never noticed? Did everyone else know this?

"What barber do you go to?" he pressed.

"I usually cut it myself," I stammered back, my cheeks flushing. The boys laughed in unison, taking turns touching my forehead.

"Makes sense, then," the boy said, motioning for his friends to move to another section of mirror.

I was humiliated. My earlobes burned. Tears welled up. Years of badgering to keep up a 4.0 GPA but not one lesson on how to shape a hairline and avoid being discovered as a fraud. So much time spent overachieving to prove that I belonged, and the other Black boys could spot me faking it from a mile away. And if I tried recounting what had happened to the white boys who had called me over just minutes before, they would be as dumbfounded as I was. This was the intersectional purgatory I had run away from: too white to notice that my haircut gave me away, too Black for anyone else to understand.

I shot a panic-stricken look around to see who may have caught a glimpse of my embarrassment. Conversations continued unabated. Circles of friends sat cross-legged, giggling. The clock ticked loudly on the back wall. No one looked in my direction.

Like so often before, I was alone.

~

I was just over two years into my new career and had already managed to get a promotion. I had gone from a musty fur costume to a much cooler pair of shorts and a thin polo shirt. The more consistent schedule of the parades meant that I could pick up a second job at a nearby Starbucks. I would get up long before the sun rose to open the shop, busying myself with lattes and cappuccinos for a few hours, then change uniforms in the parking lot behind the strip mall and speed off for my shift at Magic Kingdom.

Life was good. Stockpiled ramen noodles and expired Starbucks snacks had been replaced with the occasional night out at our local TGI Fridays. Quarter tanks of gas became full tanks, and collections calls slowed as I gradually caught up on payments. But money wasn't the only thing trending in the right direction. I had begun to settle into my new home. I had coworkers who looked forward to seeing me every day and a designated spot to sit in the break room. I found dance classes to attend after work and a local bar that would slip me one extra drink after last call. And for the first time since sneaking out of my parents' house in high school, I had friends and places to be until the wee hours of the morning.

I never got *the talk*. Black parents in the United States sit their children down to warn them of the unjust pitfalls that await them, how they can try to safeguard themselves, how to avoid—and survive—encounters with the police, especially after dark. *Keep your hands on the wheel. Don't reach for the glove box. Keep your voice down and be respectful.* But *the talk* doesn't happen at white dinner tables. It doesn't have to. So just as I had taught myself about sex through AOL chat rooms, I taught myself that certain streets are not safe to walk at night, that I would draw unwanted attention in certain parts of town, and that I had to drive under the speed limit on policed side roads.

These aren't the same life lessons that my siblings were forced to learn. Their pale skin gave them a free pass, and I bet such things never crossed their minds. Our dinner conversations were sterile: monotonous chatter about English class, the details of a recent party. Still, I managed to pick up some important lessons through osmosis, unknowingly armoring myself with snippets gathered in passing. Much of these sounded more intense than necessary. I had always been the subject of stares and hushed whispers, but I had never felt particularly unsafe around police officers. They were billed as friendly stewards of neighborhood peace, and I almost never interacted with them outside of a hometown parade or a passing greeting at the city library. Nevertheless,

I absorbed *the talk* subconsciously, the stories of other kids imprinting on my brain. I was lucky they did.

It was just after two o'clock in the morning, and I was on my way home from performing my rotating designated-driver duty. I didn't mind. It was a relief to take a night off from assassinating my liver. I didn't need to be drunk to enjoy a night out with friends, and I hated the idea of anyone getting behind the wheel under the influence. I've always been concerned with making sure that everyone gets home in one piece—and not in handcuffs.

The frost had just finished melting from the windshield of my truck as I crossed into Windermere. Cold days are rare in Florida, and my battered old Mazda Navajo was struggling. The seats didn't lock into place, which meant pressing my left foot firmly against the footrest to keep the cushion beneath me from launching forward with every press of the brake. The lights in the console were dim and flickering, an irritating light show dancing across the dash. Hot air blasted from the vents, pushing the chilly air out through the worn window seals. I cranked the handle, trying to close the window as tightly as possible, but the whistling of an icy breeze through the crack continued.

Windermere is a sleepy suburb of Orlando, best known for its sprawling golf courses and exclusive gated communities. Tall concrete walls shield homes owned by the likes of Tiger Woods and other conspicuous celebrities from the curiosity of the outside world. It's a fascinating place to drive through if you have time to stop and gawk at the impressive mansions and tightly manicured lawns. I've rolled through the accessible neighborhoods daydreaming about what it must be like to never worry about where your next meal is coming from, whether your car is safe in the parking lot, or how to avoid being late on rent . . . again.

I rounded the corner that marked the halfway point of my drive home. It was a familiar landmark. The road bent at a nearly ninety-degree angle, a dangerous trap for anyone not paying attention. The street itself was narrow and lined with trees, and wispy branches hung like a canopy overhead. I yawned, trying hard not to doze off behind the wheel. Though I didn't mind being the designated driver, I didn't love staying up later than everyone else and driving while trying not to fall asleep. A pair of headlights appeared in the rearview mirror. There were rarely other cars on this stretch of road so late at night, and the sudden appearance of this one caught me off guard. I tilted the mirror to avoid the glare and noticed the hood of the car dangerously close to my bumper.

I glanced down at the dashboard to confirm that I wasn't going too slow. Nope. Right on target. I slowed and edged toward the shoulder to let the car pass, but it continued to hug close to mine, its tires flirting with the edge of the road. Alarm bells began to sound in my head. Contrary to popular belief, Florida is not merely a monolithic collection of the world's wildest headlines. Like much of the country, it is a melting pot of people and ideologies. Though a skinny queer kid might be safe enough waiting for a taxi on Ocean Drive in Miami Beach after the club has emptied, in other places he doesn't dare stop for gas once the sun has gone down. That truth takes on a new shape when the skinny queer kid is Black.

The headlights flashed, high beams clicking on and off frantically. My eyes darted from one side of the road to the other, searching for signs of someone awake to help. Dark porches and long driveways stared coldly back. I slowed further, my heart nearly exploding out of my chest. Without warning, red-and-blue lights atop the car ignited, their rotating glow illuminating the inside of my truck.

Breathe. You're fine.

The engine growled and sputtered as I slowly rolled to a stop. I carefully cranked the window handle and kept my right hand on the steering wheel. Manual windows were a conundrum. I knew that leaving my hands on the wheel was important, but screaming at an officer through my closed, foggy window was sure to arouse suspicion. I took the risk of lowering it gently. I instinctively scanned the passenger seat discreetly to make sure that I didn't have something incriminating. I didn't smoke weed and had nothing but a half-empty bottle of water and a dirty pair of sneakers in the car. Nevertheless, my knee-jerk reaction was a panicked scan for anything that might get me dragged from the rusty truck by my neck and tossed into the back of a cruiser. A pair of footsteps crunched over the gravel alongside me, stopping at my open window. I turned my head and came face-to-face with the Windermere PD.

"Good evening, Officer," I said, unable to mask the tremble in my voice.

I immediately felt silly for having reacted so anxiously. She didn't look threatening at all. Her face was kind. Her expression, soft and understanding, was punctuated by a pair of black-rimmed glasses. Her dark brown hair was pulled back and clipped tightly into place. Her uniform was crisp and freshly pressed. She stood stiffly with her hands clasped in front of her.

"Do you know why I pulled you over?"

"Um . . ."

I racked my brain for the right answer. I knew I wasn't speeding because I had looked down to check twice. If anything, she had been speeding, barreling down on me in her souped-up Dodge Charger. I had been wearing a seat belt and watching the road diligently. Though I was tempted to give her the answer I assumed she was looking for, I knew that admitting anything I wasn't guilty of would only get me in more trouble.

"I'm honestly not sure," I replied quietly. "I'm sorry."

For the first time since approaching the truck, she looked more closely inside. Her eyes surveyed the back seats and the mat on the passenger side. The torn headliner fluttered in the cold breeze, catching her attention briefly. She looked the vehicle up and down, peering methodically, before looking back at me. Her invasive gaze scoured my every inch, from the top of my head to the tip of my sneakers. The club was always warm, so I had dressed appropriately, despite the unusually bitter cold. A thin white tank top hung from my collarbones and hit at the thighs of my shortest pair of shorts. They extended only a few inches from my waist, leaving my thin, hairless legs visible down to the rims of a pair of black ankle socks. I shuffled my feet nervously. By the time she finished checking out the truck, the kind expression on her face had melted away. Her lips were pursed with disgust, her squint narrow, her brow furrowed.

"Why don't you tell me where you're coming from?"

My heart was beating so loudly that I wondered if she could hear it too. I knew what she was implying. Here I was, in cutoff booty shorts and a woefully inadequate tank top, driving a decaying old truck through an affluent area long after most people had gone to bed. Everything about me was conspicuous, a reason for suspicion in her mind. Forget the countless times I had driven this route or my frequent stops at a nearby park to read books in the serenity of the lakeside grass. To this cop, I didn't belong. I was out of place. I knew that she didn't need a credible excuse to accuse me of driving under the influence and slap a pair of handcuffs on my wrists.

"I was taking a few friends home," I said in response to the stiffness of her scowl. "I'm the designated driver tonight."

The officer sighed heavily, now visibly annoyed. "I'm going to need to look inside the car."

Maybe there are those who would have quietly obliged, sitting awkwardly in the driver's seat while she rummaged through cup holders in the back. And perhaps I should have just invited her in. After all, I had nothing to hide. But something about it didn't feel right. I was terrified and shaking, but I still had enough wits about me to know that the officer was flexing her power unnecessarily. There was no need for her to look in my truck, and I was not going to give her an opportunity to "find" something that wasn't there to begin with. She still had not told me what I was being pulled over for, and her previous scan through the windows cast no doubt on what I'd just told her. On top of that, I couldn't shake the way her demeanor had changed. The softness in her face had hardened into a grimace. The patience in her tone had evaporated. She looked me up and down as if repulsed. So I reacted without considering the consequences. I broke the rules of *the talk*.

"I don't think that's necessary," I blurted.

She scoffed audibly, shifted her weight, and reached for the door handle.

"You don't have a right to be in here, and I would like you to stop," I said, with more force than before.

She stared at me in disbelief. I later came to the conclusion that she was stunned by having been challenged by someone she doubted had the guts to swat a fly. Time stood still. We stayed locked in an unwavering glare, each waiting for the other to stand down. After a long, painful pause, she huffed angrily and retreated to her vehicle. Under normal circumstances, I might have felt relief. She had wanted to make a point and failed. I exerted my right to privacy and succeeded. But this encounter wasn't nearly over. She hadn't yet told me I could leave, and the lights atop her car still blazed furiously in my rearview mirror.

Regret sank in. The situation was devolving into one of the horror stories I had overheard growing up. A Black guy gets pulled over in some unnerving part of town where he isn't welcome. Tensions are high. He's nervous. The police officer is jumpy, often drunk with perceived power. The guy loses his cool. Takes his hands off the wheel. Talks back. And before you know it, he's either in the back seat of the police cruiser or being zipped up in a body bag. I knew the horror stories well, but I had never imagined *how* someone would find himself in such a scenario. *All he had to do was comply.* That's the standard line I had heard at the dinner table more times than I could count. It sounded reasonable enough to a kid scooping peas under a napkin to avoid eating them. But now, on a dark, winding road in the dead of night, a terrified kid was caught in the ire of a scorned police officer because he dared to challenge her self-important assertion of power.

After a while another car arrived. The second cruiser roared onto the shoulder, flinging gravel behind it. The wildly twirling lights of the two cars were dizzying. A pair of large men climbed out of the second car and began conferring with the officer who had pulled me over. By now, what little heat there had been in my truck had escaped into the night air. I realized my hands were still clamped to the steering wheel, shaking uncontrollably. My teeth chattered, and my thighs vibrated against the worn fabric seat. I might have started to cry if the cold air hadn't dried up my tears.

The largest of the officers approached the truck. His arms were big and intimidating, each at least twice the size of my leg. Veins bulged from the forearm he planted on the sill of the open window. His partner stood just a few feet behind him, near the rear corner of the truck. His flashlight beamed fiercely into the windows, another attempt to intimidate me. The largest officer stuck his face in the open window and snarled.

"You want to tell me why you were disrespectful to the other officer?"

I wanted to scream at his patently absurd accusation. I had been extremely respectful from the beginning, answering her questions honestly and politely. If anything, I deserved an explanation for why I had been stopped in the first place. I wanted an answer as to why I was still sitting on the side of the road, cold air blasting through the window. I knew my rights. They didn't have a reason to be in my car, and I had a right to know why I had been pulled over and what prompted the call for backup. I had seen that change in an expression enough times to know what she was thinking. She didn't like me—not just me as an individual, not just the sarcastic tinge to my tone, but people *like me.* I wanted to scream it all at him. But calling my parents for bail money was a nonstarter. So I gritted my teeth and spoke slowly.

"I apologize if she felt I was disrespectful," I mumbled, my hands clenched tightly to the steering wheel. "But she still has not explained to me why I've been stopped, and she has no right to be in my truck."

The largest officer's already short fuse shortened even more. "You need to step out of the car," he barked.

I would have jumped to comply, but my feet were paralyzed with fear. Had I heard him right? Did he tell me to step out? Is this how it starts? Is this how I end up on the front page? Who calls my parents to tell them I've been shot? My breathing became shallower, my voice veering toward hysteria. "Again, I apologize," I stammered. "I'm happy to take a ticket for whatever I've done and handle it first thing in the morning."

"I said get out of the car," he snapped.

I popped open the door and slowly planted each foot on the gravel below. They buzzed painfully, sharp tingles exploding from each toe. The cold wind licked my bare skin, raising the hair on my legs. My entire body shook uncontrollably from a debilitating combination of the cold weather and the terror of what might come next. I turned and faced the side of the truck, staring at my stunned reflection in the glass. In a matter of minutes, my calm drive through a familiar neighborhood had become the recognizable prologue to a police-brutality nightmare. It was almost unfathomable that any of this could be happening to me. They didn't care that I had no criminal record and didn't pose a threat. I had challenged their authority. And for that, they were determined to punish me. The silhouette of the officer grew in the reflection until he stood just a few feet behind me.

"Put your hands on the car," he said, whirling on his heels again and marching angrily toward his own idling vehicle. "Fucking faggot."

That's the last vivid part of the encounter, the last memory that clearly reverberates a decade later. *Fucking faggot.* The rest is mostly a shapeless blur. Time moved slowly or quickly or not at all. The wind was roaring or rustling or eerily still. I can't remember enough to piece together a coherent picture, just shattered fragments, like the surface of a broken window. I've heard that the mind naturally blocks out parts of traumatic experiences, a reflex designed to shield us from things that will continue to damage us long after they've passed. Perhaps mine walled off the rest of that night for good reason.

I do remember that it felt like hours. My toes went numb, despite me wiggling them discreetly to keep them awake. I remember the officers' raucous cackles as they sat on the hood, letting me shiver. They wanted to teach me a lesson. I remember them combing through every inch of my truck, despite my earlier protests. And after they found nothing and gave me permission to crawl back into the front seat, humiliated and chilled to the bone, I remember the woman's face. She smirked, proud of what she had accomplished. She wanted me to know that she was more powerful than me. She wanted me to know what she thought of people who dared to question her. She wanted me to know that faggots weren't welcome in a neighborhood like that one.

"Your tags are expired," she said, thrusting a hastily written ticket at me. "Drive safely."

~

If the intent of that encounter had been to teach me a lesson, it failed. I was enraged and emboldened. I had moved more than three thousand miles from home, with no friends or family to fall back on. I had no flush savings account or deep-pocketed people to call, should I find myself in trouble. Everything about what I was doing was inherently risky. And no homophobic slur from a hotheaded police officer was going to strip me of my courage.

I put on a freshly ironed T-shirt and stepped outside to wait for my ride. A few months had passed since the encounter with the cops, the jarring memory now slightly dulled. I had been invited to a club downtown by a few people at work. I knew nothing about the club, but the way they had described it in the break room made it sound magical. I grew up sneaking out to a dingy nightclub in downtown Portland. It wasn't pretty. The inside was run-down, the juice bar staffed by a sour-faced, underpaid college dropout. To keep the doors open to anyone over sixteen years old but under twenty-one, they didn't serve alcohol. That didn't stop people from drinking, though. Teenagers guzzled warm bottles of vodka in a nearby parking garage, vomiting into trash cans on the walk to the club. Thinking back on it, the entire business model was ill advised. At the time, it just felt like a scandalous place to escape from under the thumbs of our parents. But a dark club full of drunk, underage boys and the lascivious stares of older men who had stumbled over from nearby bars was a recipe for predatory disaster. I hoped this club would be nothing like that.

We parked on a side street underneath a tall fluorescent lamp. The neighborhood was cute, totally unlike the part of town we lived in. My apartment was in the sprawling suburbs near the theme parks, a vast swampland dotted with cookie-cutter complexes and sliced up by highways. But this part of the city was residential and quaint. The streets were narrower and broken up by patches of cobblestone. Small bunga- lows were tucked behind carefully manicured lawns and freshly washed sidewalks. The humid night air was punctuated by the hum of insects and the occasional hiss of a sprinkler. No loud rush of traffic or bright lights from a nearby fireworks display. It was peaceful. It reminded me of home. Though I knew I couldn't afford it, I imagined it would be nice to live in a neighborhood like this someday.

We sauntered up to the club, a towering black building set back a bit from the road. It was out of place on the block, its ominous-looking walls stretching up into an optical illusion created by dramatic lights beaming up from the ground. Brilliant blues and purples danced across the dark, textured paint. A cyclone fence ran along the edges of the property, in stark contrast to the pristine picket fences of the neighbor- ing houses. A muffled thump of bass rattled the glass door. I tugged on the handle and slipped inside.

A gruff security guard patted each of us down before we piled a crumpled wad of bills onto the counter. The frustrated drag queen on the other side snatched it, stuffed it into the squeaky drawer of an old cash register, and shooed us through the doorway. Beyond was a laby- rinth, each room buzzing with a different vibe. In one, slow R&B beats played as a couple of scantily clad dancers wound themselves around a pair of poles along the wall. In another, a rap track boomed, and bodies pressed close to one another. I was definitely out of my element. Unlike the drab juice bar in Portland, this scene was all grown up. Skirts were shorter, the music uncensored. The men were tall and fit, bulging biceps filling every sleeve. The atmosphere suggested intoxicating danger, as if we had descended into the cauldron of the seven deadly sins. I stuck close to a friend, clinging to his shoulder as we snaked our way toward the bar.

Beyond the sexier lyrics and better-stocked bar, something more striking differentiated this club from the one I was used to back home: I wasn't the minority. Every corner contained a sea of Black faces, beautiful shades of melanin milling through the haze of fog machines. I had never seen so many people who looked like me in one place before. I was simultaneously fascinated and utterly overwhelmed. Those who spend most of their lives in the majority don't understand how disorienting this can be. To them, it's commonplace to look around and see reflections of themselves staring back. For me, it felt forbidden, as if at any moment my elementary-school teachers would barrel through the front door, shout at me to hike up my pants, and drag me out by my ear. I looked up at the club's name, emblazoned on a glowing sign behind the bar: PULSE.

As a kid, I was always acutely aware of being the token Black person. It was impossible not to notice being the only one, everywhere I went. I got used to being asked if I ever thought about playing basketball and having to fend off aggressive attempts to touch my hair. It became second nature for me to explain my entire family tree to those who couldn't wrap their minds around my brother's blond hair. Still, no matter how many times I wished to be around more people like me, I had never considered what it might feel like to be in the majority. I beamed as we wound our way through the vast structure.

I was grateful to my friends for having brought me on this dizzying new adventure. I needed to keep a close enough eye on them to know when it was time to pile back into the car and start the trek home, but

I also had an urge to explore. I wanted to see what was tucked into the farthest corner of the dimly lit patio, to sip a drink and watch the dancers from afar, to disappear into the crowd, soaking up my first experience of being surrounded by other faces like mine. I wanted to know what it felt like to be invisible and unremarkable, even if just for a night. With my friends busy at the bar, I took the opportunity to slip away, melting into the abyss of writhing bodies.

There's something undeniably beautiful about blending in. I had never wandered the confines of a nightclub without getting at least a handful of double takes or seeing nervous men instinctively place hands on their wallets. All my life, I had been made to believe that I was something to be hidden away or overcome. I was told to avoid hip-hop music, the gateway to delinquency. I had long internalized the idea that only a select few Black men can be physically attractive, while the rest of us were relegated to the friend zone. But before me was an ocean of beautiful Black people, gyrating their hips to the beat, carefree and full of life, everything I'd worried I couldn't be if I embraced the truth of who I was. I let the natural flow of the people carry me from one space to the next. I ordered a drink at every bar, just to have an excuse to meet the bartenders. I sat on the patio and peered up at the stars, grateful to have been given this unexpected experience. I weaved my way to the center of the dance floor, content to let the sway of the crowd spin me in circles.

Eventually, the heavy pours caught up to me, and the walls began to rock back and forth a little. I made my way to a white leather couch near the VIP booths and flung myself down on a thick cushion. Things were spinning gently, so I closed my eyes and took a few deep breaths to regain my sense of equilibrium. When I opened them, I was no longer alone on the couch. A tall man was sitting next to me, peering down.

"I promise I didn't pass out," I stammered, tripping over my words.

"I just wanted to make sure you were good," he replied.

As his face came into clearer focus, I realized he was stunningly beautiful. His eyes were large, brown, and gentle. His brilliant white smile flashed between sentences, deep dimples forming each time. He had smooth skin that radiated in the colorful lights. I wondered if he was gay but was too nervous to ask.

"Was that a no?" he asked, a perplexed look falling over his face. I had been so caught up in drooling over him that I wasn't paying attention to a single word he said.

"I'm so sorry," I said. "I didn't catch the question."

"I asked if I could kiss you," he said, smirking.

Before I knew what was happening, my lips were pressed against his, which were softer than I had imagined, and he used them gently. The sweetness of his cologne wafted between us, tempting me closer. It occurred to me that I had never been approached in a club like this. And he was certainly the most beautiful man to ever ask me for a kiss. An instinctive nervousness crept through my stomach. My usual reaction would have been to stand up awkwardly and get as far away as possible. I wouldn't have known what to do with someone like him. But he kept one large palm wrapped firmly around my thigh, his grasp too firm to slip away from. I would have to be brave and go with it.

He pulled his lips from mine and gazed longingly at me. His face glowed in the low light of the bar. "Tell me," he said, "do you like to dance?"

I nodded silently, desperately trying to contain my excitement and hoping he couldn't see the blush barreling from one ear to another. I had no idea what kind of dancing he expected and was genuinely concerned that my alcohol intake might cause me to topple over without warning. But I didn't know when I might get another opportunity like this: a beautiful man inviting me to curl up in his arms and get lost in the rhythm of the music.

He slipped his fingers between mine, pulled me to my feet, and tugged me under the disco ball.

CHAPTER 4

DREW

Our world is designed for extroverts. We place a high value on those with a seemingly effortless knack for socializing. Magnetic personalities are deified, while the more muted among us are bulldozed in conversation. We turn every email into a video call and race to fill silence with sound, indicting quiet as "awkward" without considering its necessity. Anyone who prefers solitude and a good book over the relentless calendar of a socialite is looked upon with pity, as if we don't crave nonstop interaction because we're just weird. The exaltation of extroversion is so pervasive that, until very recently, I identified as an extrovert by default. On the surface, I check all the boxes. Public speaking comes naturally. I take charge of group projects. I can play the role of "life of the party" without much effort. And in my experience, those aren't just helpful qualities—they're necessary. But those were acquired skills for me, the learned behaviors of someone trying to excel in an extrovert's paradise. On the inside, I'm an introvert.

Small talk has always induced anxiety. The mere thought of sitting across from someone at a table, locked in a complicated tango of getting to know them between awkward pauses, makes my palms sweat. That's especially true when the "someone" in question is a cute boy. For years, I watched in jealous awe as my friends serial dated with relative ease.

They seemed to know all the right words to say, at exactly the right times. They never tripped over their tongues the way I did, stumbling through basic interactions like a circus clown with two comically large left shoes. They burned through first dates like wildfire, getting off on the thrill of the social experiment itself. I, in contrast, have always been an interpersonal nervous wreck.

I was enraptured by Drew from the first time he appeared on my Instagram feed. His boyish charm and innocence beamed from my phone screen, a mischievous glint baked into his smile. His feed was chaotic and carefree, a haphazard collection of family photos and goofy mirror selfies taken with an oversize Canon camera. I don't know how I first stumbled across his profile, but I was immediately enamored. By all objective measures, he was very attractive. Dark brown hair in turbulent spikes. Golden brown eyes that seemed to radiate when the light hit them just right. His face was youthful and bright. But beyond the standard measures of beauty, there was something deeply intriguing about him. Drew's personality leaped through the screen, resonating with authenticity. He was often wedged between friends, a gangly arm draped around someone's shoulder and a cheesy grin plastered on his face. His selfies were moody and pensive, but his photos with others were joyous, his radiant energy electrifying everyone around him. I was immediately drawn to him. He looked happy, genuinely happy. The kind of happy I had envied in the other kids at school when both parents cheered them on at a soccer game. The kind of happy I tried to fake at work, my singsong voice masking annoyance at customers' complicated orders. Drew was full of the happiness that I didn't think people *like us* were supposed to feel. It was intoxicating.

I sat up straighter in bed, squinted intensely at the screen, and hovered over a picture of Drew gazing into a mirror. I was convinced, by now, that I'd casually stumbled upon my future husband. Which made the next steps obvious. I imagined which of us would take the other's last name. Debated which picture I'd use for his contact profile in my phone. Would I put him under "hubby" or "bae"? I made a short mental list of potential baby names—you know, just in case. The more I scrolled, the more fascinated I became.

Drew had pictures with his mother dating back years. I wanted to know more about her. What was it like to have her around during the awkward phases of middle and high school? What was it like to have her there at his graduation? When he bought his first car? Other pictures featured a diverse collection of friends, an array of shades and identities. What was it like to be so unafraid? I wanted desperately to ask: *Do security guards stalk your friends through the aisles of Target too? How do you find the courage to slide into your skinniest pair of jeans and strut out the door unashamed? Is your forced smile a mask, like mine? Or do you mean it?*

A mutual friend's name grabbed my attention mid-scroll. An old roommate. He had liked a few of Drew's photos and bombarded them with a string of emojis. *This is my chance,* I thought.

I took a deep breath and sent a virtual SOS: I need a favor . . .

~

One successful method I've found for tamping down my paralyzing shyness is practicing small talk in a long, narrow mirror in the corner of my bedroom before having to execute it for real. I was so intent on scoring a date with Drew that I hadn't even considered what I would do if my maneuvering worked. Hours before meeting him, I stood in my usual practice spot, wobbling awkwardly in a tight pair of black boxer briefs and staring at my bony reflection in the smudged glass. I grazed my collarbone with one hand, thinking about all the times my thin body had been a crippling source of insecurity. I had been told to "eat a cheeseburger" so many times that it was like a constant drumbeat in the back of my mind, its volume almost deafening at the most inopportune times. My gaze dipped down, now fixed on my bare toes wiggling on the carpet. Maybe if I just went to the gym and added a few extra pounds . . .

Focus, I scolded myself, lifting my eyes to the mirror. *He's going to ask you what your favorite color is. The answer is green.* I shifted a little, sucking in my stomach and puffing out my chest. *He's going to ask you what your favorite food is. The answer is tacos.*

I fumbled with the small plastic buttons of my shirt, unfastening them with trembling fingers, then slipping my arms through the arm-holes. My stomach churned disapprovingly. What if he rejected me? What was my exit strategy if the conversation tanked? How would I respond if he laughed uncontrollably at my awkward attempts at conversation and charged out the door before the server could refill our water glasses? I took a deep breath and shook the doubt from my head. Drew seemed different. And I didn't need to get in my own way.

Dusk light fell across the busy parking lot as I found a spot a few hundred feet from the door of the restaurant. I carefully calculated that the ideal location for my car would be just far enough away that I could go unnoticed while giving myself a last-minute pep talk in the rearview mirror but close enough to the entrance that a panicked sprint after a conversational face-plant would put me behind the steering wheel before Drew could catch up. I gazed anxiously into the mirror.

You can do this, I whispered softly. *You deserve this.*

His silhouette was visible through the tinted glass of the tall front doors. He was unassuming, his shoulders slightly slouched. The outlines of his arms and legs were disarmingly awkward and gangly. One hand grasped an oversize martini glass. I tugged on the long copper door handle and slipped inside.

Drew's energy was more electric than I had imagined. He bounced excitedly from the plush cushion, coming within inches of my face and nearly launching his cocktail into my crisply pressed shirt. "Hi!" he said enthusiastically.

I gulped down my nerves. "I think I need a drink too," I murmured.

I was already enthralled. Drew was effortlessly remarkable. He glided through casual small talk without hesitation, his boyish giggle bubbling up from time to time. His lips danced from frenzied descriptions of his latest anime obsession to shallow sips of his drink without missing a beat. I was surprisingly calm, the warmth of his confidence providing shelter from the insecurities clamoring in the back of my mind. He was so interesting that I forgot to stress about the way my left sleeve came unrolled every few minutes and whether my cologne was still strong enough. Drew was a breath of fresh air. Comfortable. A fountain of joy and energy.

A mischievous look washed over his face. "Okay, I have a question for you," he said, his gaze narrowing.

Ha! Do your worst, I thought. *I've been preparing for this.*

"What are your thoughts on the for-profit health-care system in America and how it impacts us as consumers?" he asked, his face tightened into a serious expression.

I nearly blurted out "GREEN!" before I realized what he'd said. Every date I'd ever been on had the same basic formula: A nervous greeting. Unbearable small talk. Long bouts of silence over a meal. An awkward hug goodbye, capped off by a flush of embarrassment as I saw him pull up Grindr before leaving the parking lot. Those copy-and-paste first dates never asked me anything memorable, and they certainly didn't ask for my opinion on an issue both deeply personal and politically contentious.

My mouth hung slightly open, the insides of my lips drying in the faint stream of air from a nearby vent. Was this a trap? Was he purposely baiting me? Trying to embarrass me in a crowded restaurant? Or was he really curious about what I thought? I took a long swig from my glass, its contents coating my tongue and spilling warmly down my throat. Liquid courage is a hell of a drug.

"Ugh, a mess," I stammered. Before the words had finished tumbling from my mouth, I dropped both eyes, bracing myself for Drew's laughter, or at least an audible scoff. I was mortified. I'd had all day to rehearse carefully crafted small talk and make myself sound smarter than I actually was—the consummate conversationalist. But all that preparation had resulted in only a silly response to a serious question.

Drew's unrelenting grin grew wider. He wasn't laughing or rolling his eyes. There wasn't even a hint of judgment. His face was innocent and curious, urging me to go on. As a server guided us to our table, I rambled a bit more about the grotesque American health-care system, its levers of power designed to enrich a handful of greedy white men, literally at the expense of our lives. Drew nodded slowly, allowing me to string together incoherent thoughts without interruption. I locked eyes with him and listened intently to his thoughtful response. He worked in health care but never let his insider knowledge devolve into condescension. The conversation meandered lazily from topic to topic, pit-stopping at systemic racism and sidewinding into the cost of higher education. On the third visit from our annoyed server, we hadn't stopped long enough to take a breath, let alone glance at the menu.

Somewhere between sopping up pools of soy sauce with steamed dumplings and digging into a large bowl of white rice, I learned that Drew was half Finnish and half Japanese. He binge-watched an anime series I couldn't pronounce, and he rattled off a litany of character names so long I could hardly keep up. He was an EDM enthusiast, gleefully boasting about his favorite DJs and reliving live sets with wild gesticulations. He was defiant and proud, detailing his latest failed fling without lowering his voice to avoid the prying, potentially homophobic ears of nearby diners.

Drew's long, gently crossed legs were squeezed into a pair of skinny jeans. They were the kind of jeans I had often tried on in the quiet safety of a retail fitting room but reluctantly placed back on the shelf to avoid an inevitable side-eye in the checkout line. He was everything I'd been afraid to be. Brazen. Unapologetic. Queer. A man living at an intersection of races and unashamed of his natural femininity. And his silent courage was somehow contagious.

By the time the check arrived, I realized I hadn't once glanced over my shoulder before talking about an old boyfriend, a reflex born out of fear of being overheard. I had forgotten to stiffen my wrists and churn the gravel in my voice, pieces of armor I'd long adopted to avoid piquing the interest of wandering eyes and ears. I had ordered a fruity cocktail without first considering who might snicker when it arrived, pink and frothy with a vibrant flower floating elegantly on the surface. Drew's lack of inhibition dared me to act the same.

We kissed that night. He offered to drive me to my nearby parking spot, so I slid into the front seat. He drove a gray Volkswagen Jetta, the pungent scent of crayon wax wafting from inside as the door swung open. Before I could click the seat belt in place, Drew's face was smashed against mine. His lips were soft, and he smelled faintly of sweet cologne and sautéed onions. The satellite radio was tuned to electronic music, the mesmerizing thump of the bass radiating in the firm leather seat beneath me. I was so nervous that I wedged one hand underneath my leg to stop it from trembling and squeezed my eyes closed. My mind was racing frantically from one insecurity to the next. *Do I smell okay? Could he tell I had no idea what I was talking about when he brought up affordable housing? I should have brought gum.* The boys I liked almost never liked me back. And they certainly didn't make the first move on me in a dimly lit parking lot. I shifted in my seat to quell my anxiety. Drew pulled his lips from mine and smiled.

"I had a nice time tonight," he said.

I agreed, popped open the door, and scurried out of the car before he could change his mind about me. I caught myself doing a joyful skip, tried to course-correct, and stumbled, nearly careening into the tinted driver's-side window of my car. Blushing, I turned and waved nervously to assure Drew that I was fine. I eased into the soft leather seat and exhaled loudly.

Nailed it.

~

Daddy issues do a number on guys like me. We spend an entire childhood chronically overachieving and perpetually terrified of failure, desperate for affirmation that isn't coming because we don't play baseball or bring home pretty girls. An entire childhood seeing the things we can't change about ourselves painted as "less than" by a world obsessed with traditional displays of masculinity, then a tireless fight to overcompensate for them.

"Man up!" fathers will say at the first sign of tears after scuffed knees, foisting their own decades-long emotional repression onto the next generation. Magazine covers and Instagram feeds silently reinforce that if we aren't blond with blue eyes and six-packs, we should be grateful for the opportunity to look on in amazement, ashamed that we're too lazy to look the same. It's a toxic soup that leads to unhealthy expectations for interpersonal relationships with other men, and an inability to appreciate the various forms they take. In short, we're so desperate to be seen as and wanted by men that their desire becomes the only aspect of a relationship we can imagine. It's a running joke inside our community that gay men can't officially call themselves friends until they've slept together, as if no friendship can exist outside the murky confines of sexuality, as defined by everyone else. I hate tropes like that because they don't leave space for the myriad lived experiences that make up our community. But if I'm being honest, I also really hate how close to home they hit.

Despite what I'd thought was a perfect first date, Drew's romantic interest didn't extend past our passionate front-seat rendezvous. He let me down fairly easily, insisting that we be friends. I obliged, masking my disappointment with a few heart-eyed emojis, and slid into the friend zone with oft-practiced ease, attending parties and joining game nights without letting on that I hadn't shaken my boyish crush. I laughed as expected, publicly shrugging off his rejection when well-meaning strangers remarked that we were a cute couple.

But it stung. I'd spent so many years relegated to the friend zone that it brought a familiar roller coaster of emotions. Frustration that I'd done everything I could and still came up short. Embarrassment that I'd allowed myself to be so vulnerable with someone who never saw me as anything more than another addition to their circle of friends. Relief that I wouldn't have to perform encores of the first-date tap dance followed immediately by a wave of sadness that I still wasn't good enough.

~

Brink was one of our favorite nightclubs while it lasted. Most queer spots in Orlando are just outside the busy confines of downtown, tucked away in more sparsely populated parts of the city and inaccessible without a car or a rideshare. Brink was the exception: a bustling venue in the heart of downtown comprising two buildings and a busy, open-air courtyard wedged between them. Clubgoers lined up on a crowded thoroughfare to flash their IDs, then disappeared behind a tall black fence into the recesses of the club. To the left, scantily clad boys crowded the narrow walkway surrounding a sprawling bar. Muscular dancers snaked across the bar top, stopping periodically to gyrate on a wooden box or peer down and entice a handful of crumpled bills from an onlooker. Inside the other building was the dance floor, a dozen strobe lights pulsating hypnotically until the early hours of the morning. The bar in the back served the strongest cocktails, which made it our traditional first stop. We spent countless nights there, clumped under the lights, whirling wildly from one corner to the next. We made new friends outside, under the glow of a streetlamp, and said goodbye to old friends just before the sun peeked over the horizon. Brink is also where Drew and I had our first fight.

Hours earlier, I had learned that Drew was hooking up with a mutual friend. They'd spent the night together on more than one occasion. It shouldn't have upset me, but it did. I was embarrassed that I had bought Drew's excuse about not being ready to jump into a relationship, and I was jealous that someone else in our circle was good enough when I wasn't. I was bitter that I now had to pretend like nothing was wrong while I watched them sip drinks and giggle together. But I was determined to get through our Friday night without an ounce of this showing on my face. I slid into a pair of jet-black jeans and gazed into the mirror, tugging angrily at a small crease at the bottom of my shirt and huffing at the way it perched atop my love handles. *You're gonna have to fake it better than that.* I forced my pained grimace into a smile, stepped into the doorway, and flipped off the lights.

I stopped ordering fruity cocktails not long after my twenty-first birthday, substituting their nauseating sweetness with drinks that got straight to the point. Long Island iced teas and tequila sunrises gave way to whiskey neat or top-shelf vodka with a splash of seltzer water. This started off as a move to save money on bar tabs, but I also discovered the added benefit of fewer morning-after headaches. The trade-off was that a particularly potent vodka soda shortened the road to a flared temper and words drenched in regret.

We sauntered up to Brink's front door a few minutes before midnight. We had downed our usual pregame drinks and piled into Ubers from across town. The bar was less busy than usual. My nervous reflex was to guzzle one cocktail after another. We rotated around the space, stopping to catch up with familiar faces we hadn't seen since last week's outing.

"Oh, hey girl!" someone shouted from across the bar, beckoning us closer. We ambled over slowly, careful not to appear overly eager.

"Heyyy," we replied in unison, the elongated vowel sound like an aircraft marshal guiding us into an awkward side hug.

We washed and repeated that routine half a dozen times, moving from one area to another, making frequent pit stops for our favorite bartenders along the way. With each drink, my frustration bubbled closer and closer to the surface. Drew and our mutual friend were as friendly with one another as always, but a lens of jealousy had fallen over my tipsy gaze, and all I could see was two secret lovers conspicuously dangling their new fling in front of me. They sped off, giggling quietly and glancing back over their shoulders at us. I imagined they were laughing at me, poking fun at my sour expression and how silly I had been to think I could end up with Drew. I imagined that the entire group quietly pitied me behind my back, afraid to tell me how pathetic I was. My blood simmered.

Keep your cool, I thought to myself as we stepped out into the dancing strobe lights.

I had just sipped the last drops of liquid in a small plastic cup when I turned and saw them dancing together. That wasn't abnormal. We all danced with each other. In fact, one of my favorite things about becoming proudly queer was brushing off the misogynistic stigma around being playful with other men. We frequently pulled each other close, twirling until crashing into a nearby table and doubling over with laughter. No one expected a bunch of gay guys to put on a tough, masculine exterior and maintain a safe, heteronormative distance. Everything about our flamboyance was normal. But the alcohol coursing through my veins, and the jealousy brimming just under the surface, clouded my judgment. My emotions boiled over.

"I don't want to be your friend," I blurted to Drew, tears welling on the rims of my eyelids. "I can't be your friend."

He stood in stunned silence, occasional flashes from the brilliant white strobe lights illuminating his wide eyes. I could see he was embarrassed and hurt—a predictable response that could have been avoided had I stopped to consider my words before I let them fly from my mouth. The group peered awkwardly at us, waiting to see who would crack the thick tension.

I shouldn't have said it. Words matter, and I have spent my life preaching that we should choose our own intentionally. It wasn't as if I didn't enjoy Drew's friendship. I did. And I wanted to keep making fun memories together. But his rejection had stung. And a friendship didn't feel sustainable if I was going to spend it jealous and hurt that he didn't want to date me. I desperately scoured the recesses of my mind for what to say next. By that time, a few tears had spilled onto my cheeks, which made me more embarrassed and enraged. Before Drew could utter a response, I whirled on my heels and darted out the door into the night.

~

I pulled into a parking spot near the entrance of a vegan Chinese restaurant in the heart of the city. Drew and I had been there at least a dozen times together, almost always finding our way back to the same plush vinyl booth under a window just a few steps from the front door. We had made countless fond memories there. Drunk nights stuffing fried rice into our faces and laughing until our sides hurt. Picking up takeout to scarf down while watching an old movie. It became one of our staple spots, a place I looked forward to going every time. Except this one. I was nervous. An intense knot was buried in the pit of my stomach as I put the car into park and turned off the headlights.

Drew had asked me there to talk. Any other friend probably would have avoided the conversation, content to sweep it under the hangover rug and pretend like nothing happened. But Drew was unlike any other friend I had acquired. For starters, he was more confrontational than anyone else I had met, not shy to jab a scolding finger in the air and interrupt with a contrary opinion. But somehow that made him more endearing. He embraced necessary confrontation because he cared, and he shared his perspective because he trusted us to respect it. Apathy or disinterest on his part would have been a far more damning sign than a request to meet up for dinner in the midst of a fight. Which meant that he still cared enough to talk it out.

I pulled open the front door, ringing the small bell hanging above it. Only a few tables were occupied, all by couples locked in hushed conversations over steaming plates of fried rice. Drew sat in our usual booth, eyes down, poring over his phone. My heart was pounding in my ears, and I briefly considered getting back in the car. But I willed myself forward, shuffling my feet toward the table and sliding into the seat across from him. He looked unfazed by our altercation earlier in the week, his demeanor measured and calm. We made small talk about work, friends, his upcoming vacation. By all accounts, he seemed to have forgotten our reason for meeting. I was more than content to leave it that way.

Drew selected a handful of vegan appetizers while I zeroed in on an entrée. The move was calculated on my part. More food meant less time to talk about the feelings I hadn't yet found the words to articulate. Cramming my mouth full of food was the surest way to get out of there without having to confront the awkward reason for our rendezvous. The server brought over a few ceramic plates and two sets of silverware, then refilled our glasses of water. Drew took a sip from his glass and cleared his throat. When he parted his lips to speak, the words were slow and deliberate.

"Seems like we have some things to talk about," he said.

I squirmed in my seat. The words I had used that night in the club were harsh, and I didn't mean them. My feelings were hurt, and I was deeply jealous, yes. I was frustrated with myself for liking him more than he liked me. But the hardest part about trying to unpack it all was that it went much deeper than that. The whole thing exemplified all the struggles I had with men growing up. My unrealistic and unhealthy expectations weren't Drew's fault. He was just suffering the consequences of my decades-long fear of inadequacy.

I didn't know how to be friends because I had spent so long internalizing the idea that being friends with another gay man was just the consolation prize for not being worthy of his romantic interest. I didn't know if I really wanted to date Drew or if those feelings were born from my desperate hope that he valued me as much as I valued him. I had trouble identifying whether I loved the idea of being his boyfriend or just loved the idea of being someone's boyfriend. I didn't know how to begin neatly packaging all of those thoughts for his consumption, but I knew that in order for us to create something meaningful, to have a shot at salvaging the best thing I'd ever stumbled into, I was going to have to find a way to put them into words.

"I shouldn't have said those things," I replied. "I do want to be your friend."

My mind raced for what to say next, where to begin. But before I could start explaining the deeply embedded insecurities standing in my way, Drew interrupted.

"Before we go there, I need to apologize," he said. "I knew that there was an imbalance in our relationship, and I didn't respect how my actions might make you feel. You had every right to be upset with me, and my only hope for tonight was that you'd give me a chance to start over."

I half expected to see hidden cameras suddenly revealed, to see someone pop out from behind a swinging door and announce that I was being punked. I had been so nervous for this conversation because I felt ashamed that I was fundamentally broken. And that my self-doubt had manifested as anger toward someone I cared about. I came in expecting to beg for forgiveness, fully prepared to be turned away, like every other time when one of my unhinged outbursts imploded a promising friendship. I had imagined that Drew would spurn me, tell me that I desperately needed help, then storm out of the restaurant and never speak to me again. Instead, *he* was asking for forgiveness. His brow was furrowed, a deep concern twisting his face.

It struck me that I was experiencing something new. Drew cared for me. He loved me. Not in the way I had drawn up while scanning his Instagram feed. Not in the ways that I had learned to measure my own value, reducing interactions with other men to a scorecard of physical attraction. Drew loved me more deeply than that. He saw me as a confidant. An accomplice. A brother. And judging by the worried look on his face, he was even more terrified than I was that the damage might be irreparable.

I met his gaze from across the table, fidgeting with my fork. "So," I said with a sheepish grin. "Should we start over . . . friend?"

All the anxiety of that week melted away, our nervousness fading into giggles as we stuffed our faces with some tofu concoction and chilled sesame noodles. For most of my life, the word *friendship* hadn't had this kind of meaning. I had friends, of course. My little cohort of high school pals got me through some of the darkest parts of my childhood. The roommates and coworkers I had collected in Orlando made me feel more at home than I ever had in Oregon. But this person—this *friend*—was different. He wasn't wary of my short fuse or discouraged by my abrasiveness. He didn't run from the dark echoes of my past. He embraced them and accepted them as a personal challenge. It was like he could see past every layer that had hardened around my core over the years, straight to the essence of who I was.

Drew didn't want to be my friend because he needed something from me. And his offer to continue building a relationship wasn't a consolation prize for someone he deemed unworthy of his affection. To Drew, friendship was more than those things. It was the most valuable connection he had to offer, the highest honor. Boyfriends come and go. Biological families can be toxic. But for Drew, friends were forever. From the first day we met, he had decided I was going to be a part of his life, no matter what. I was too blinded by my own insecurities to see it, but he had chosen me as family before the appetizers ever hit the table. His brother. His friend. And the prospect of losing that so terrified him that he dragged me to one of our favorite spots with the sole intention of apologizing for hurting my feelings and ensuring I didn't get away.

I let out a quiet sigh of relief and took another bite of my dinner. I figured I could handle friendship after all.

~

People have all sorts of reasons for falling in love with certain holidays. For some, it's the heart-shaped boxes of Valentine's Day, filled with chocolates of all shapes and flavors. For others, it's the twinkling lights of a Christmas tree, crisply wrapped presents stacked underneath, and the welcoming of family from all corners of the country. I admit to putting Mariah Carey on repeat the day after Thanksgiving and delighting in the search for gifts at the outlet mall, but holidays have always been hard for me. Stemming back to the time I was made to feel unwelcome at home one Christmas break, the seasons that fill others with joy have always made me feel like a nomad, a transient soul, hopelessly alone. Every holiday except one: New Year's Eve.

It's cliché to pin all your hopes, dreams, and aspirations on the day we crack open a new calendar. Like so much else, New Year's Eve is an invention based on a rudimentary, self-obsessed understanding of how the universe works. The infatuation with the start of a calendar year is little more than a human need for milestones, a catalyzing cosmic reset. But we *are* human.

Drew shared my affinity for this season of new beginnings. As we put our bags in his trunk, I thought about how he had warned me not to overpack for the short trip to Fort Lauderdale. Of course, I had heard that as a challenge to pack more. Drew didn't follow his own guidance either. We were never prepared to go on vacation without at least two pairs of underwear for each day we'd be gone. I wedged my bag in next to Drew's and closed the lid.

The ride to South Florida was long and uneventful. My mind wandered. I thought about the lowest point in my life, another New Year's Eve under far different circumstances. I thought about downing liquor in Ben's apartment, the ceiling swirling above me as I tried to keep myself from getting sick on the carpet. I thought about how isolated I had felt that night, surrounded by people but hopelessly alone. I glanced at Drew out of the corner of my eye, his head bobbing along with the music. It was nice not to be alone anymore. And remarkable how different life was now that I felt safe living it.

My reset with Drew took our friendship to new, once unimaginable, heights. We spent nearly every waking moment together, out at the club until the sun peeked over the horizon, then commiserating by the pool a few hours later. I didn't have to try so hard around Drew. He didn't wrinkle his nose when something came out of my mouth the wrong way or scoff when I admitted some embarrassing secret. We had a level of comfort with one another that was almost disorienting for me.

I had always envied, despised, or lusted after the other gay men in my life. This was much more enjoyable.

We pulled into the parking lot of our crappy motel, and I began lugging our bags through the dilapidated lobby and up to the room. Drew was humiliated that his insistence on frugality had left us in a less than ideal part of the city. The window of our room had been screwed shut, its view an overgrown field where trees and shrubs tangled with tall clumps of grass. Beyond it, trailers and tents were scattered haphazardly across well-worn dirt. Drew pushed past me and pulled the curtains closed.

"We should have a drink," he snapped.

The space was small and dated. Two narrow beds were pushed together against one wall. The carpet was worn and dingy, a visible path ground into the fibers. Drew whizzed by me, furiously pumping a bottle of cologne, trying desperately to mask a musty, nauseating combination of mildew and stale cigarette smoke that both of us were too embarrassed to explicitly acknowledge. The whole scene had the feel of an '80s horror film, and I half expected someone to leap from the rickety closet doors with a butcher knife as soon as we shut off the lights.

Drew poured a couple of drinks, just a little stronger than usual. I sipped mine quietly and discreetly checked under the covers for signs of cockroaches. The accommodations may have left something to be desired, but I was happy to get away from home with my best friend. He had begun planning weeks in advance, and the evening was tightly choreographed, in typical Drew fashion. Just after sundown, a few of us piled into an Uber and headed to dinner. Despite having the most cumbersome legs, I was relegated to the back seat, where I struggled to hear the conversation over the blaring music.

Dinner was mediocre, but the company made up for it. The long table in the back of the restaurant was packed with friends old and new. We made chaotic rounds of introductions, and thanks to Drew's heavy hand at the hotel, I was tipsy before we sat down, which made socializing easier than it might have otherwise been. More than once, I caught myself slowly gazing around the table, wondering how the hell I had ended up there. For much of my young life, I had assumed that I would be dead by twenty-one. I had no real basis for that assumption, just an irrational fear of dying from AIDS and an inability to imagine myself beyond the struggle to make ends meet. Yet here I sat, surrounded by the smiling faces of other misfit toys, casually ringing in a new year, as if this had been the plan all along.

Drew finished shouting a short toast and lifted a brimming champagne glass. The tiny bubbles burst to the surface, sparkling in the lights of a nearby lamp. "Here's to friends," he said elatedly. *Clink.* To friends.

The club was already buzzing by the time our Uber pulled up to the curb. The line moved rapidly as security staff herded people in sequined blazers and skintight dresses inside. The bouncer slapped a wristband on my arm, plucked a crisp ten-dollar bill from my hand, and shoved me toward the open door. If Drew hadn't practically funneled alcohol down our throats, the chaotic throngs of people being jostled by irritable staffers might have been enough to put me right back into a rideshare and speeding to the hotel.

I stumbled inside and let my eyes adjust to the low light. The club was enormous, its vast open spaces broken up by bar tops and clusters of seating. A gaggle of tipsy friends huddled around a cocktail table off to our left, surveying a Grindr profile on someone's phone. In the center of the room, a large, round bar was fully stocked, rows of liquor bottles glistening in the overhead lights. A long hallway led to a busy patio in the back. A tall pergola covered the space, string lights twinkling between the slats. Across the concrete pad, another hallway wound back inside the club, past a pair of narrow bathrooms and into a cavernous dance hall. Some rickety stairs with a wobbly railing rose to a deck that looked down onto the stage.

It was a lot to take in. We had gone to big clubs before and been packed like sardines into rowdy crowds dozens of times. But this took it to another level. I may not have identified as an introvert in those days, but I still responded to overstimulation like one. On nights as busy as this one, it was typical to find me making a beeline for a quiet corner and burying my face in my phone until I had managed to suck down my second drink. But Drew's heavy pours and the buzz of New Year's Eve pushed me deeper into the crowd, one hand clutching the shoulder of the person in front of me. I didn't find myself annoyed by the occasional drunk girl careening into me before bouncing down the hallway. I wasn't bothered by the tedious pilgrimage from one side of the club to the other, squeezing and winding my way through the gyrating mob of people. Maybe it was the change of scenery or the quality of the company, but my shoulders felt more relaxed. There was no tension in my neck. I felt like I could be loose and uninhibited. I slid up to a handsome bartender and ordered another drink.

"Make it a double."

That night was a blissful blur. We drank until we slumped onto a cushioned bench to catch our breath. We laughed until our sides ached. We picked up flimsy paper props from a folding table and did impromptu photo shoots on the patio. I vaguely remember the clock striking midnight, my lips locked with those of a beautiful stranger who disappeared into the crowd before I could ask his name. We made fools of ourselves, spiraling from one side of the club to the other, shrieking whenever another of our favorite songs came on. We hugged over and over again, our inhibitions replaced by unfiltered displays of affection. I recall, through the mental haze, launching myself into the back seat of an Uber and diving face-first into a bag full of Taco Bell. That's where the memories finally trail off, the fragments fading to black.

I don't remember what resolutions I made that year. Knowing myself, they were likely quantifiable, pragmatic. *I want to go to the gym at least twice a week. I want to double my savings account balance by year's end. I want to score an interview for that promotion by the fall.* For better or worse, I have always defaulted to the practical. After years of dinner lectures about fiscal responsibility and 401(k) balances, I can't help but lean on the tangible. But once in a while, in the safety of my own mind, I dare to dream. I don't remember the resolutions, but I remember watching my friends, chaotically ping-ponging from one end of the club to the other, and dreaming of what the years ahead might look like. A decade's worth of New Year's Eve celebrations. Weddings and birthday parties. Brunch cocktails and quiet movie nights at home. Unhindered by others' assertions that the world would never be ready for people *like us*, I dared to dream about the future. It felt good.

By the time I woke up, the sun was beaming through the open window straight onto my face. My head was pounding, and my stomach was doing backflips. Visions of Fireball shots and tequila chasers danced behind my eyelids, threatening to toss the whole night up all over the bedsheets. I cracked one eye open and surveyed the scene. One friend lay in the other bed, loud snores emanating from a blanket tossed over his head. Wrappers were piled on the bedside table, napkins doused in hot sauce spilling onto the dingy carpet. It all stank of stale liquor and body odor, exacerbating the waves of nausea washing over me. I slipped my feet out from under the comforter, stepped onto the grungy carpet, and pulled on a T-shirt.

Coffee.

Drew was sitting on a plastic lawn chair in the motel's courtyard. His gaze was glassy and fixed on an imaginary point in the distance. He still wore his shirt from the night before, the buttons now fastened askew, deep wrinkles crunched into the fabric. I shuffled over, collapsing into the chair next to him, and let out a heavy sigh. The courtyard was quiet and peaceful. The thick, humid air was still, the palm fronds above our heads undisturbed. Neither of us spoke for several minutes, content to allow the pounding in our heads to rage on uninterrupted.

There's something special about the people with whom you can enjoy silence. Something necessary. So much of our time is spent filling the silence with noise. We play background music and incessantly murmur among ourselves. Some of it has value. But much of it is to ward off our dread of silence. Our darkest thoughts live there. Our fears of inadequacy lurk in the shadows of quiet reflection, a truth we avoid by filling the world with sound and distraction. We live petrified that if our thoughts are allowed to come into clear focus, we won't be able to stomach how they appear. But occasionally you meet someone with whom you can traverse the treacherous waters of silence. Someone with whom you can sit, content in stillness, and simply be. Someone with whom the world needs no distraction or white noise. This is a relationship to cherish.

Drew finally turned and let out a groan. "I feel like shit," he growled.

"If it's any consolation, you look like shit too," I fired back.

A pregnant pause followed. I thought I might have responded too gruffly, my sarcasm biting just a bit too hard for his short, hungover fuse. Then Drew's laughter cut through the silence. He was nearly doubled over, gasping for air as his shoulders shook uncontrollably. Only he thought I was that funny. And only he was unfazed by the dryness of my humor.

"Thanks, you look great too," he managed once his giggles had subsided.

Silence returned, and then the only sound was the hushed whispers of occasional passersby. I treasured quiet moments like this, but they were infrequent. We spent most of our time surrounded by other friends, hordes of boys, each shouting at the top of his lungs in order to be the loudest voice. We packed nearly every minute with socializing. It wasn't often that we got a chance to sit in one another's company without having to compete with the deafening thud of a speaker or the rowdy clamor of a restaurant. Drew broke the silence again.

"I hope you know that you're my best friend," he said quietly, staring down at his feet.

"Yeah, yeah," I replied dismissively. "You too."

Drew lifted his head and looked at me with an uncharacteristic determination. "I'm serious," he urged. "People throw that term around all the time. It loses its meaning at some point when you do that. But when I say it, I mean it. I hope you know that you really are the best friend I've got."

I sat quietly, staring at a small pebble in front of my feet. I was uncomfortable. This wasn't how things had ever gone for me before. Try as I might to sabotage our relationship, Drew just kept coming back. Despite my furious outburst at Brink and my awkward apology over Chinese food, he never once stopped trying to pull me closer. I had spent my life pushing people away, walling myself off to avoid getting hurt. I was so terrified of feeling rejected and abandoned that I couldn't bring myself to accept what he was offering unconditionally. I didn't think I deserved it, and I was petrified of having to give it up someday.

But he kept on, unabated. Each time I tried to nudge Drew away, he hugged me tighter. Each time I tried to detonate our connection, he reforged the bond. It was the kind of thing I had seen families do for one another, refusing to be sidelined by bumps in the road. It was the kind of relationship that I had always secretly envied but been at a loss to create for myself. It was love. The kind I had convinced myself the world was never going to be ready to show me.

"Well, I hope you know you're my best friend too."

~

Being a best friend is not unlike accepting a promotion at work. It comes with important responsibilities. And when I commit to taking on responsibilities, I give them everything I have. I'll take over driving duties midway through a road trip without a single complaint. I'll throw a few bottles of champagne in a reusable shopping bag and be at your door in a minute when you find out the love of your life has cheated on you. I'll crawl out of bed, put on oversize sweatpants, pick you up from the county jail, and make sure you get a hot meal before taking you home. (That's a story too long for this chapter and probably better saved for another book.) But there is no more important role for a best friend to play than protecting you from your own worst instincts.

I was skeptical when Drew first started dating Juan. My skepticism stemmed from the way he was introduced to us. A few of us friends had gathered in Drew's apartment and were sitting in our usual spots. Music videos and old coverage of Eurovision, the ultra-flamboyant European singing competition that gave the world ABBA and Celine Dion, played in the background. I was engaged in my standard preparation for a night of overstimulation and loud voices, having retreated to a muted corner of the living room, where I buried myself in something interesting on Facebook. In the kitchen, Drew was mixing cocktails and recounting a recent trip to Tampa. He was at the height of his obsession with music festivals, so he was frantically reenacting all the juiciest parts of the shows he had seen and the people he had become fast friends with. His personality was almost offensively magnetic, and he was rattling off a dozen names that none of us would remember by the time the story was over. Somewhere between adding ice cubes to his glass and topping it off with a splash of soda water, he casually mentioned a boy he had met there. My ears perked up instinctively.

"Anyway, he was cute but so annoying," Drew explained nonchalantly, swirling the drink in front of him. "He just kept following us around, no matter where we went."

And just like that, he bounced to the next unlikely character in the story, breezing past this mystery boy. An unknowing fly on the wall might not have put two and two together and wouldn't have noticed the handful of seemingly insignificant details. No one else batted an eye. This one anecdote was part of a much longer story, wedged in between salacious details about his weekend. But I knew Drew better than that. He was nothing if not intentional. Mentioning this boy was significant, and he wasn't telling us the whole story. He was, in his way, slowly preparing us for greater exposure to this mystery boy down the road.

I didn't press him on it then, but I did squirrel that tidbit of information away, sure that I would need it later on. I didn't mention it to anyone else, as other friends would likely accuse me of being paranoid or finding drama where there was none, but I figured I would hold on to it just in case. Sure enough, the mystery boy appeared at a party a few weeks later.

A few of us sat around our favorite table at a bar in downtown Orlando. We had spent countless Sunday afternoons there, sipping bottomless mimosas until we could barely keep from teetering off the stools. I can neither confirm nor deny that on a handful of occasions, someone did eventually tumble from their perch and prompt our early exit. This time, we were celebrating Drew's birthday. A gregarious, extroverted only child, Drew commanded attendance at his parties without having to ask. His birthday was a highlight of everyone's year and seemed to carry on for weeks in a marathon celebration that required a strong liver and a knack for pacing oneself.

This birthday was no different. We had already completed several events by the time we found ourselves at Ember in front of a sea of half-empty glasses. We took turns making the pilgrimage to the bar for another round while the rest of the group grew louder and louder at the table. We had been there for a few hours when an unfamiliar face sidled up. Given Drew's natural magnetism, it was commonplace for people I didn't recognize to appear out of nowhere, so I initially wrote off this awkward stranger as someone who had finally worked up the liquid courage to come and say hello. Practically everyone in the bar was lining up for a selfie with Drew. I carried on laughing and talking, expecting the boy to grow tired of watching Drew flirt with everyone else and wander away. But he didn't move. He remained firmly planted at one end of the table, waiting quietly. In one hand, he clutched a small bouquet of balloons and a little gift bag. I shot him a side-eye, but he was unfazed, surrounded by an air of confidence and swagger.

Strangers don't bring presents.

Drew deftly maneuvered around the table, gesturing wildly as he told one story after another. An oblivious bystander wouldn't have picked up on the subtle cues. Drew performed nonchalance effortlessly. To the untrained observer, he seemed to be socializing innocently, sidewinding his way through adoring friends to make sure everyone felt special. He was an expert host, uniquely skilled at making every person feel as though there was no one else in the room. But his body language told me what was happening. He moved more hurriedly than usual, repeatedly glancing at the mystery boy standing patiently at one end of the table. Drew shirked embraces from hook-ups past that he normally would have welcomed with both arms. And when he finally arrived at his destination, he tossed his arm around the boy's shoulders, pulling him into a hug that was just a bit longer and tighter than usual. I glowered at the two of them suspiciously, quietly proud of myself for having picked up on the clues from the outset. Drew inhaled nervously and gestured toward the boy with his free hand.

"This is Juan."

~

I performed all the tasks of a dutiful best friend. I spent the rest of that afternoon largely ignoring Juan, despite him sitting just a few feet from me at the table. He nervously sipped from a glass and looked for someone to make conversation with, but I kept my back toward him with a chilly shrug. Occasionally I would end the stalemate to whirl around and grill him: how old he was, where he went to school, how he and Drew had met, when his last hookup was. I tried catching him off guard to see if he would slip up and give me something I could use to dismiss him as a potential suitor of Drew's, but Juan remained steady and warm, parrying each invasive question and answering confidently without skipping a beat. I nicknamed him "Juan 2012," a jab at his high school graduation year and the fact that he was at least a decade younger than Drew, and it stuck, becoming his moniker for months afterward. I poked fun at his squeaky giggle and questioned his choice to wear cargo shorts to a gay bar. I expected that, at some point, he would grow weary of my hazing and wander off into the crowd, never to return. But he didn't budge, matching my sarcastic prodding blow by blow.

It wasn't that I didn't like Juan. He was charming and handsome, with perfectly manicured facial hair and dark, brooding eyes. A mole on one cheek gave his face character, and he hid his braces by keeping his lips pursed mischievously. But being protective of my best friend was my responsibility, and I was deeply skeptical of anyone who made it past the first line of defense. He probably wouldn't admit this, but Drew's taste in men had always left something to be desired. Things seemed to start out well enough, but before long, our group of friends would get a dramatic download over a glass of wine around his kitchen island, and we'd frantically remove the boy in question from our social media accounts. Too often, people saw Drew's warmth and generosity as an opportunity to take advantage of him. He was kind; they were manipulative. He was forgiving; they were greedy. And I saw it as my responsibility to prevent him from falling into that trap again.

I did everything I could to test Juan's resolve. But he wasn't like the other boys who had so failed Drew. He was gentle and sweet, speaking softly and putting hard work into connecting with our group. He was passionate and affectionate. I had never seen anyone stare at Drew with such adoration and awe. Juan would snuggle up to him in public as if no one could see them. That would have terrified me, but Drew's face beamed every time. Juan's voice jingled with a relentless joy that, from anyone else, would have annoyed me to no end. But somehow, with him, it was disarming. He was unflappable and determined, hyperfocused on studying for classes and committed to the gym twice a day. He was wise beyond his years and fiercely opinionated, working himself into a tizzy explaining things like which brand of peanut butter worked best in a smoothie.

If each of them was remarkable on his own, together they were magical. Their energies were distinct but similar, humming in perfect harmony. From the first day, they finished each other's sentences and seemed to understand one another, sometimes without having to say a word. They listened to the same music and fell in love with the same movies. They found quiet corners at parties and curled up in each other's arms. Like a cosmic collision, Drew and Juan were meant for each other. They were almost symbiotic, two intended souls that had finally bumped into each other unexpectedly. It was clear from the start that they were hopelessly in love, and though I tried to keep up my skepticism for as long as possible, it was undeniable that Juan made my best friend better.

I supposed I'd have to find space in my heart for them both.

PART 2:
A WORLD UPSIDE DOWN

CHAPTER 5

THE LAST NORMAL DAY

I tossed off the blanket and slid my feet onto the cold hardwood. My head was pounding from half a dozen glasses of champagne the night before, as if my brain would explode through my forehead like a firework at any moment, and I could feel the blood throbbing in my toes. I sat hunched over the edge of my bed, ushering a few deep breaths in and out, trying desperately not to vomit. Drowning my recent breakup with a boy named Eric in a bottle of drugstore sparkling wine had seemed like a solid plan. Now my thumping temples begged to differ.

I peeled myself from the sheets, stumbled to the living room, and sank onto the couch next to a basket of clean laundry. Years of my parents waking me up on weekend mornings to clean toilets and wash dishes had left me incapable of lying in bed on weekends. Dad was notorious for providing us with no more than two chances to rouse ourselves before he'd return to flash the lights on and off obnoxiously or splash cold water on us until we relented and climbed out of bed. And I could almost hear my late mother's stern voice scolding me: *Brandon Joseph—headache or not, you need to get up and get moving.* I glanced down at the heap of crumpled T-shirts and grimaced.

The clothes spilled over the edges of the basket, a few lonely socks scattered beside it. I bent over to pick up an unmatched pair, and a sharp wave of pain rolled through my head, begging me to find a better distraction. Maybe getting a leg up on the competition that Drew had challenged me with. He was the nerdiest person I knew. He could ramble about an anime series he'd discovered on Netflix without stopping to take a single breath. He hosted an annual watch party for Eurovision, complete with a neat stack of printed brackets and brightly colored cocktails. And he loved anything sci-fi—*Star Wars*, *Battlestar Galactica*, *Star Trek*. He and I were locked in a tense race to see who could binge every season of *The Next Generation* first, with bragging rights at stake. I didn't much care for *Star Trek* and couldn't name more than a handful of its characters, but I couldn't pass up an opportunity to best Drew on his home turf. I stuck a toe through a hole in the laundry basket and tugged it closer, the pair of jeans on top teetering precariously, then flicked on the TV.

Maybe I can get a few episodes ahead, I thought.

Life was so . . . normal. The kind of normal I'd craved as a kid. The kind of normal I'd only seen afforded to classmates who still had both parents around and neighborhood kids who never had to explain why they looked "exotic" to a crowd of curious preteens. The kind of normal with breakups, best friends, broken hearts, lazy days, and mismatched socks. There, nursing a grueling hangover and carefully balancing a leaning tower of underwear on the edge of a cushion, I was unexpectedly living the life I had spent years envying from afar. It wasn't nearly as glamorous as I had imagined, but it was mine. There were no luxury cars or complimentary club memberships, but there was stability. And safety.

My phone lit up, briefly pulling me away from the bridge of the starship *Enterprise*. A new photo of Drew and Juan on Facebook. They were almost offensively cute together, that couple who stole every ounce of attention before making it two steps through the door, the pair of friends whose magnetism makes others simultaneously jealous and awestruck. And they worked in perfect tandem. Juan disarmed with a contagious giggle and innocent charm. Drew grabbed attention with a mischievous smirk and mesmerizing curiosity. I often found myself watching them operate, both enamored and annoyed by how effortlessly they moved together. They were a team, a naturally infectious combo. And they were, in many ways, what I'd hoped Eric and I could be. I let out an exasperated sigh and hit "Like."

Morning gave way to afternoon, and I made my way to the pool deck. The midday sun blazed unrelentingly, its rays dancing on the water's cool blue ripples. The heavy summer air slowed the beating in my temples, if only just a bit, as cicadas droned hypnotically from the trees. My mind drifted back to the picture of Drew and Juan, embracing each other excitedly in front of a roller coaster. I wasn't just jealous of the love they shared and how nauseatingly photogenic they were. I envied that it all seemed to come so naturally to them. Their relationship wasn't bogged down by the debilitating insecurities I'd grown accustomed to, which always seemed to leave me with another ex. They weren't constantly fighting over who lingered too long in conversation with a bartender or arguing about which of them had left the coffee mug in the sink. There was no deep, corrosive, mutual mistrust, just a vulnerable willingness to leap into the abyss together. They were recklessly in love. Unafraid of failure. Happy.

I was furious at myself for daring to believe that Eric and I could achieve the same. And it wasn't his fault that we hadn't. I had an uncanny knack for dragging out my own baggage at the most inopportune times, sabotaging anything remotely joyful, and retreating behind walls I'd built around myself over the years. I couldn't let Eric love me the way I wanted because I still didn't believe that I deserved to be loved. Every time his eyes met mine, I saw my flaws in their reflection. The way my smile sags on one side. The little boy who had never really grieved the loss of his mother. The puffy bags under my eyes, gifts from my mom's side of the family that have always made me appear a few years older and a bit more tired than I should. The terrified college boy who snuck out of Ben's apartment, violated and alone. I couldn't meet Eric's gaze without questioning how I'd even caught his attention in the first place.

Drew and Juan affectionately fawned over one another, and I wanted that kind of boyish passion but couldn't begin to figure out where to start or how to believe I was worthy of such a love. The weight of the muggy air overtook me.

My phone jolted me awake. I glanced around, a little dazed, unsure of how long I had been asleep. The sun had drifted into the horizon, casting vibrant oranges and purples across the sky, and the buzz of cicadas had subsided. The water in the pool was still. On my phone, a text message from Eric: I want to go out, but I don't have anyone to go with.

My heart pounded. My fingers trembled over the screen. The throbbing in my temples returned. Going out with Eric that night was a terrible idea. I was still nursing a brutal hangover. I was in a very vulnerable state, and diving headfirst into those murky emotional waters again was ill advised. At best. But a piece of me wanted things to work. And humans are nothing if not susceptible to the allure of the familiar. I rationalized it by telling myself that maybe seeing me one more time was all Eric needed to realize our potential. After all, there was something different about him. Something . . . possible.

I'll go, I texted back, shoving aside the doubt lurking in the back of my mind.

Good friends show up to celebrate all your triumphs. They shed tears when you read your wedding vows. They're there for the baby shower. They're a reliable source of affirmation when everything seems to be going right. Best friends show up when everything is going wrong. They answer a collect call from the county jail and raid their coin jars to help get your car out of the tow lot. They help you change a tire on the side of the road, pick out a suit before a funeral service, offer a hand so you don't have to be alone. Best friends are there when no one else is. They're also expected to be there when you make a half-baked decision to hang out with an ex. So I called for reinforcements.

Eric wants to go out . . . so now I need you there as well, I texted Drew. I don't want to be alone.

Are you sure that's a good idea?

No, I'm not. But it's happening.

Okay. We will be your support.

I blame my grandmother for my insistence on having a spotless home when I welcome guests, even if they've been over countless times before. Grandma's house was notoriously clean, a minefield of spaces off limits to muddy shoes and chaotic children. Some of my fondest memories are of her long, meandering journeys from her perch in a plush chair across from the television to the kitchen in the back of the house. Every few feet, she would stop to pluck dark bits of fuzz from the white carpet, intent on keeping it pristine. That routine—step, pluck, step—instilled in me a deep aversion to having dishes in the sink or messy bedding when company arrives.

I raced from one corner of the apartment to the next, scooping up piles of dirty laundry and cramming them into a basket in the closet. I stashed a stack of plates in the dishwasher without the usual prerequisite rinse. Eric had been to my apartment a dozen times, but this visit felt the most consequential. How could I possibly be ready to take care of someone else if dust bunnies betrayed that I wasn't ready to take care of myself? What would he think if he walked into a cluster of empty champagne bottles, evidence of my attempts to wash him from my mind? There was a light rap at the door, and my heart skipped a beat.

Here goes nothing.

"Painfully awkward" doesn't begin to describe it. Eric walked in first, hustling past me into the bedroom to change his clothes. Drew and Juan barreled through the front door a few minutes later. The tension was so thick that everyone was swimming in it. Juan tried a handful of jokes, only to watch them fall flat as Eric stared at his phone. Despite his best efforts, and mine, nothing could ease the paralyzing silence.

Drew trusted me with almost everything in life—except control of the cocktail shaker. To this day, I have a talent for pouring particularly potent drinks that burn just a little too much going down. Drew learned early on that allowing me to play bartender results in a painful morning after, so more often than not, he would casually appear in the kitchen just as a group of friends needed a refill, commandeering the vodka and saving everyone from an overpoured disaster. I slipped behind the bar and began aggressively filling a glass when he shot me a glower from across the island. He was silently imploring me to ease up. Our gazes locked briefly before he finally relented, my pained expression prompting him to cede the refuge of the kitchen to me. I gulped down a round as Drew and Juan requested our rideshare.

~

In many ways, Pulse embodied the sense of community I had discovered after moving to Orlando. It was one of the first places where I held hands with someone I had a crush on without glancing over my shoulder first, an exhilarating act of defiance that might have put me in danger almost anywhere else. It was one of the only spaces where I dared to let my guard down, to be a little messy and unpolished, unafraid of who might be watching. Tucked off the beaten path, hidden from sight, Pulse was a place where I could be all of myself. A safe space. And if I was going to get things right with Eric, I needed that kind of home-field advantage.

Pulse also embodied the disorienting sense of normalcy I had stumbled into at this point in my life. For the first time ever, I was financially stable, had a reliable group of friends, and could dream beyond the next paycheck. Mundane moments still felt like dirty little secrets, quiet bits of freedom stolen from a world I didn't belong to. A week without checking my account balance. An apartment all to myself. These were unimaginable luxuries just a few years earlier, when I was still inventing new ways to stretch a packet of ramen noodles. It wasn't just that I'd found a tiny corner of the world where I could dance like no one was watching. Everything about Pulse embodied the kind of normalcy I had once coveted, then envied, then finally claimed as my own.

The long line to get in. The red-faced valet, beads of sweat clinging to his eyebrows as he battled the humidity to keep up with a growing line of cars. The bubbling water feature near the front door, its usual foamy cascade pouring into a shimmering pool below. The blast of chilly air when the door swung open. The frustrated drag queen perched behind a counter near the door, her intricate makeup a porcelain mask hiding deep annoyance with the parade of intoxicated boys prancing through the entrance. The barely audible tinkling of plastic beads dangling from the doorway, shrouding the dark recesses of the dance floor from view. The incessant thud of reggaeton beats radiating through the floorboards. The frenetic dance of light reflected off a spinning disco ball. The musty scent of a fog machine near the foot of a tattered wooden stage groaning under the weight of a capacity crowd. I could have navigated the club blindfolded, meandering through the tight hallways with an effortlessness born of carving out a stake in this refuge of normalcy nestled in a world desperate to rob us of it. Pulse felt more like home than almost anywhere in my hometown. We nudged our way to a sticky bar top, Eric's glower needling the back of my head.

Home, don't fail me now.

We had built a predictable routine at Pulse over the years. Saunter through the front door with unearned confidence. Boldly present a hand to be stamped for reentry. Peel back the beaded curtain. Strut to Kate's bar near the back of the club. Order our usual cocktails. Dance. Laugh. Drink. Repeat. We had performed this ritual so many times that it was almost second nature, which took a little of the edge off the night, when the group's awkwardness seemed to chill our conversations. Clutching hands, Eric and I meandered across the crowded dance floor to the bar. It was busy, maybe busier than I had ever seen it.

Eric's jaw flexed visibly, his cheek muscles flaring as we shouldered our way through the crowd. He didn't mind a rowdy environment—over the past few months, we had occasionally day-dreamed about donning our skimpiest outfits and elbowing our way to the front of the crowd at a music festival in town—but deep down, Eric was an introvert, and the chaos of the club, mixed with the tension between us, was making him visibly uncomfortable. In my fantasy, we nervously eyed one another from across a sparsely populated dance floor, irresistibly drawn to one another's arms under the disco ball. I imagined a sort of '80s rom-com plot in which time slows to a crawl, our steps punctuated by a dramatic synth beat. But reality had other ideas. A drunk girl sloshed the contents of her cup and narrowly missed my shirt. Eric was visibly annoyed and seemed to do everything he could to avoid peeking in my direction.

We ordered a round of potent vodka sodas and a couple of Fireball shots that I knew I'd choke down through a grimace. A giggle from Kate, a blurry receipt to sign. I was grateful that the drinks I had poured earlier were kicking in, numbing the sting of my anxiety. Eric looked absolutely miserable. When his eyes weren't rolling, they were frantically darting from one corner to another, seemingly searching for somewhere to hide. I wanted nothing more than to shake him and tell him how I'd moved emotional mountains to be there with him, pulling the "friend card" to get Drew and Juan out of their pajamas and into a matching pair of button-down shirts. Instead, I sipped aggressively at the thin black straw plunged into my drink, seeking relief at the bottom of a plastic cup, an escape from all the words I couldn't seem to find.

Eric broke the silence. "Let's go outside."

Spaces like Pulse become an extension of home, a place to call your own, a respite from the weight of the world. There was something freeing about the rush of the night air on Pulse's outdoor patio, the tranquil rustle of palm fronds occasionally interrupted by the roar of trucks speeding past. The patio was a hideaway where we could catch our breath, a shelter from the chaotic energy of the club. One side was uncovered, with a shallow fountain awash in a streetlamp's light. The rest was tucked underneath a large awning, with a long bar and a few seats scattered across the narrow stretch between the building and the tall black fence that shielded patrons from curious passersby.

Drew had a master's degree in clinical psychology, which meant he had an uncanny knack for cracking open the crevices of your life that you were masking from the world. He could drill down to what was gnawing at the back of your mind, deftly dodging the walls and defense mechanisms designed to keep others out, all between sips of his cocktail, and he offered unsolicited advice at random— dispensing it more frequently the more drinks he consumed. This night, he was on a tear about relationships. Frustrated by watching me sulk around our apartment complex for a week, going from one pair of oversize sweatpants to the next and shoveling pints of Ben & Jerry's down my throat, Drew ranted about the shortsighted trap of human insecurity.

"Why spend so much time agonizing over the little things that annoy you about someone rather than just appreciating how much you love them?" he questioned, shifting his gaze between me and Eric. But I knew he was talking to me.

My inability to sustain romantic relationships was absolutely my own doing. Years of having my heart incinerated by those I'd trusted had left me hasty to hunt for the flaws in others, and rather than communicate my way over the bumps in a relationship, I let the rifts pile up until I ultimately severed ties. I'd done this with every man I feared getting too close to—and I'd done it again with Eric.

Drew must have noticed the awkward shuffling of my feet, because his serious gaze gave way to a sheepish expression. "We all do it," he continued. "I just wish we'd focus more on how much we care about each other."

He was right. The world outside felt more contentious than at any time I could remember. Fueled by incendiary rhetoric, Donald Trump's inconceivable rise in the Republican Party felt like it was tugging at the seams of humanity. Already strained family relationships were teetering on the edge. Whole swaths of the country were engulfed in the flames of outrage. At every turn, it felt as if a simmering fury threatened to boil over, the bonds of shared experience straining under the weight of tribalism and a deep mistrust of even neighbors. In this context, the patio at Pulse felt simultaneously freeing and naive. We could drop the tense facade of an increasingly hostile world and talk openly about the things keeping us up at night. But there was also something oversimplified about the community we had formed there, a kind of childlike blindness to the complexities of our lives. Nothing was complicated with the mesmerizing thump of bass under your feet and a familiar glass sweating against your fingers. Everything made sense.

Drew would often gesticulate wildly when finishing a thought, his skinny appendages taking on a mind of their own, punctuating his conclusions with an index finger jutted into the air. And when it came time to hammer home an impromptu therapy lesson or pose for a group photo, he would stretch out an arm, pull someone in close, and drape it over their shoulders like an ill-fitting scarf. I never quite figured out if he did this as a sign of affection or merely to keep himself from tipping over after one too many cocktails, but I always found it reassuring.

He hooked me with one elbow and tugged me toward him, swaying gently, his arm dangling lazily in front of my chest. "You know what I wish we did more often?" he said, with a boyish innocence and a sparkle in each eye. "Tell each other that we love each other."

I barely contained an aggressive eye roll. This had been his strategy all along: the drawn-out lecture about seeing the good in others capped off by forcing me and Eric into a warm embrace. It was ingenious, honestly. And I should have seen it coming. But I'd gotten so lost in the allure of imagining the world that Drew was painting that I'd forgotten about the thick tension hanging between us.

"I love you guys," Drew pressed, coaxing the group into a messy hug that quickly collapsed into giggles. I wouldn't admit it out loud, for fear of stroking Drew's inflated ego, but he knew exactly what I needed to hear.

We locked arms and made our way back inside to dance. The door clicked closed behind us, and the darkness of the club enveloped us. The bass raged beneath our feet.

～

Just before 2:00 a.m., we convened in a dim corner to discuss our exit. Pulse had a young and notoriously rowdy crowd, with college-aged clubgoers capable of guzzling seemingly bottomless cheap liquor and still making it to class the next day. Those skills had long left us, and we knew that if we didn't get home soon, we would regret it in the morning. After a few hurried words, we agreed that Drew and Juan would finish one last dance while Eric and I used the restroom.

Moments that change our lives are often marked by an indescribable phenomenon: the vivid clarity of some memories juxtaposed against the foggy distance of others. Colors that are bright and unmistakable. Dull hues you grasp for in the back of your mind but can't quite make out. Smells that trigger a flood of emotions years later. A fuzzy, odorless background that never seems to come into focus. Perhaps it's because I've never been very good at science and don't have a deep understanding of how the brain works, but to this day, I can't comprehend why some bits of the next few minutes are so vivid that their sharpness still jolts me out of bed, while others seem trapped behind a thick fog, their silhouettes like the faint remnants of a dream.

The restroom was near the front of the Black Room, a crowded bar inside the club named for the thick, dark paint covering its walls and ceiling. A short hallway snaked around a corner, emptying into a cramped, dimly lit room with a few urinals against the wall. Because it was designed only for men, there were no stalls or partitions, which forced occupants to push closer toward the wall to shield themselves from a wandering gaze. By the end of the night, assorted liquids pooled in the corners amid an array of discarded cups and bottles. I stood in front of a urinal, gazing up at a poster.

Vivid: The painted faces of familiar drag queens peered back at me from the poster, their high cheekbones splashed with fiery reds and opulent purples. There was a party coming up, hosted by a few of my favorites.

Foggy: Was Eric at the urinal next to mine? Or was there a space between us? What did the air smell like? What song was playing? I had already forgotten the date of the party as I stepped back and zipped my pants.

A tired, dingy sink was perched on a wall near the entrance to the hallway, tilted just a bit toward the ground, as if the bolts holding it up might give way with the lightest nudge. It had always seemed out of place to me, like it was willing itself to hold on a little longer.

Vivid: A clear plastic cup rested on the rim of the sink, its contents a jumbled pile of ice chips and two mutilated slices of lime. Beads of sweat dripped lazily down its ridges, sliding off the porcelain edge of the sink and into a growing puddle on the grungy tiles below. The fruit had been mashed, its rind flayed, its flesh torn. I twisted the silver handle on the faucet and stuck my hands under the cold water.

BANG BANG BANG BANG BANG BANG

An eerie sound cut through the din of the club, loud claps ringing in my ears. I turned the faucet off and tried to make out the sound, but it was gone, replaced once again by the steady thump of bass and a soaring electronic melody. I glanced over my shoulder and made eye contact with Eric. He seemed as confused as I did. *Must be a musical malfunction,* I thought.

BANG BANG BANG BANG BANG

The sound was more deafening than before. Each concussion seemed to split the air. The music went on, unrelenting, but underneath it, a sinister silence had befallen the club—its frenetic energy had been snuffed out. Eric glanced my way again, visibly panicked.

A chill skittered up my spine, electrifying the hair on the back of my neck. Gunshots.

In an instant, the restroom was crowded with a dozen petrified faces as people crammed themselves toward us down the tight hallway.

Vivid: A girl with soft, meticulously curled brown hair sobbed uncontrollably as a friend held her tightly, trying to calm her. Neither of them could stop shaking.

Foggy: Others knelt in stunned silence, their pupils wide, their lips quivering with terror. But the rest is a blur. Did they have blond hair? Or was it brown? One might have had long, tightly clasped ponytails. Maybe another had hair buzzed to the scalp. Maybe none of them looked anything like that.

I joined the group huddled against a wall, the cuffs of our pants soaked from a murky liquid trickling along the baseboards. My toes began to tingle. My feet felt cemented beneath me.

"What do we do?" one girl shrieked, eliciting a chorus of "Shhh!" from the others, who were desperate not to be discovered. A steady drumbeat of gunshots sounded both miles and inches away, a disorienting barrage muffled by only the loud thump of my heartbeat in my head. Each concussion echoed through my legs, sidewinding up my body and then exploding in each eardrum. I didn't know how long I had been crushing Eric's hand in mine—our fingers stayed locked in a tight grip—but I was grateful he was there to hold on to.

Vivid: A tangy smell wafted in. Heavy. Nauseating. With a metallic edge that singed my nostrils. I gagged. Smoke. And blood.

BANG BANG BANG

"We can't stay here," Eric said, his panic replaced with urgent determination. "It's time to go." Most people learn how they respond to crises only when they're thrust into one. Heroes rush into danger, risking their lives to save those around them. Caretakers turn a frayed bandanna into a makeshift tourniquet or perform CPR on someone clinging to life. The dazed are immobilized, stunned shock incapacitating them like helpless deer on a dark, winding highway. I was the latter. Paralyzed.

The air hung like a thick sludge, tightening around my throat, gluing my legs in place.

I don't fear death in the abstract. I'm content with the knowledge that life eventually comes to an end, that to live is ultimately to die. Sitting in the safety of my apartment, thumbing through mindless reality television, those truths don't scare me. For years I had imagined that I wouldn't live to see my next birthday, only to be surprised when it was time to blow out the flickering candles again. So internalized was my fear that being queer meant consigning myself to a gruesome, premature death by deadly disease that I hadn't bothered to consider what growing up might mean. I didn't scribble down dreams of a white picket fence into my journal because I assumed I wouldn't live long enough to have one. I couldn't picture myself growing old with someone I loved because there was no time to consider what would never be. While others searched for immortality in spirituality or religion, I had always accepted the inevitability of death. Until it was real.

With my legs folded tightly beneath me as I sat trembling in a puddle of spilled liquor, I realized that I wasn't ready to die. I wanted that promotion at work, the chance to put on a tie every day and prove myself. I wanted to finish paying off my student loans and go shopping for a house on a quiet, tree-lined street. I wanted children and grandchildren. To slip into a tuxedo and watch from the front row as Drew and Juan exchanged vows. To crawl into bed every day with someone I loved. Life had at last become worth living. And now it was being ripped away.

The tears that had been welling up spilled over, and my breaths devolved into shallow gasps.

BANG BANG BANG

Eric pulled me to my feet. My stomach was churning. The crowd of strangers had organized into a tight line, each person gripping the hand of the person in front of and behind them. A few girls whimpered softly, their shoulders visibly shaking in the dim haze. Eric gave my hand a tug, and we stumbled out into the bar.

The club felt like a tomb. Cups littered the ground. Liquor bottles, intact but tipped on their sides haphazardly, were strewn across the counter behind the bar. A thick white cloud still poured from the fog machine. Strobe lights pulsed with the blare of gunfire. A disco ball spun slowly from the ceiling. I wanted to laugh at how out of place it all seemed. I wanted to scream at the top of my lungs.

My heart pounding, I clenched my jaw and fixed my gaze on a thin sliver of light from a door, cracked open just an inch. Had it always been there? Why hadn't I noticed it? I couldn't picture where it would lead and didn't care. It was hope.

My head swam as we barreled toward the door. One foot in front of the other. It felt like it took a lifetime to cross the room, as vignettes of my past raced through my mind with every step.

Left foot.

My cousin and I sneaking off to the doughnut shop, Aunt Pat obliviously washing dishes as we crept out the door. Hearts thudding as we crossed the railroad tracks on our bikes. Giggling. Swerving. Pink frosting on my chin. Things were easier then.

Right foot.

The nerves before my first choir solo. Butterflies in my stomach. Dad beaming with pride, a rarity. His button-down shirt tucked tightly into his jeans. He only dressed up for special occasions. I wanted to tell him I was proud of him too.

Left foot.

Grandma coming to babysit after Mom died. The commanding gravel in her voice. The warm smell of freshly baked pie wafting from the kitchen. Her strong hands plunking familiar tunes on a worn piano. The stinging smell of too much bleach in the wash. She was stronger than anyone else I knew.

Right foot.

Dad was joyful the day I stopped calling him "Troy." Mom wanted me to care for him. I didn't want to share her. The pained grimace on her face, her pleading gaze. It happened casually. *Dad.* A gleam. A softening of his scowl. *I wish I'd told him that I love him.*

BANG BANG

The din of gunshots hit a crescendo as we passed by the entrance to the dance floor. *Don't look. Don't look. Don't look. You'll never be able to unsee what's in there.* I fixed my gaze on my feet and clutched the sweaty hand of the girl behind me.

Left foot.

Right foot.

~

A rush of hot summer air blasted us as the door flung open and sweat-soaked clubgoers burst into the harsh glare of a streetlamp. In a daze, gasping for air after our frantic sprint, I scanned the parking lot. We had emerged at the front of the club, near the valet parking spots. I recognized a few of the people running past me for cover. The cute guy I had passed near the bar earlier, now drenched in a dark liquid, his mouth agape. The short girl who had bumped into me by the patio an hour or so before, her arrogant scowl having faded into a panicked grimace. A haunting scream wrenched my head to the left. Someone bounded over a bush near the edge of the parking lot, his shirt soaked in blood. It was chaos—a scene from some cheesy horror film or a war documentary. I wanted to breathe a sigh of relief, but I worried that if I opened my mouth, I would vomit all over the asphalt.

The sound of gunfire ebbed then, dulled by the towering club walls and the painful ringing in both of my ears. I was dazed, shaking uncontrollably, unable to calm my trembling hands. But somehow, I was alive. Eric pulled at my elbow, urging me to keep moving. I stumbled a few steps forward and collapsed, the world knocked off its axis. I glanced down at my body for the first time, half expecting to see a bullet-ravaged mangle of flesh. I exhaled sharply. Not a scratch. I tried again to stand and promptly slumped back to my knees. My legs were like gelatin, and something gnawed at the back of my mind. A shiver ran up my spine. The hair on my neck stood upright again. Something was wrong.

BANG

I gasped. Drew and Juan were still inside.

CHAPTER 6

A BROKEN HEART

My apartment was filled to capacity, people squeezed like sardines into the tiny studio. Several hours had passed. The world had awoken to our nightmare, and the shock was settling in. To distract myself, I tried counting the number of times the door opened and closed, but eventually I lost count. My friends and acquaintances spoke in hushed tones, each visibly exhausted from a sleepless night. They rotated, making pit stops to peruse the fridge for snacks, huddling near the TV for an update, and stepping outside to make hurried phone calls and snag a few breaths of fresh air. Furniture was sparse, so people created makeshift places to squat. One friend perched on the arm of my worn brown sofa, its tired frame straining under the weight. I'd found it next to a dumpster the year before, a relic from the days when one extra item in my grocery cart could have tipped my bank account into overdraft. Another friend leaned against the kitchen island with a cocktail in his hand, gazing blankly at a peeling corner of the molding. He stirred the shrinking ice cubes mindlessly, their tiny tinkling like a faint melody over the tense murmur of hushed voices. No one cared that he was drinking at ten o'clock in the morning. Time seemed to be standing still anyway. Occasionally, a phone rang, jolting everyone back to reality and prompting a panicked shuffle. An unnerving restlessness radiated through the group, an unspoken terror that, without warning, our friends' names would appear on the list of victims.

I picked up my phone, desperately hoping to see Drew's name. I played a hopeless game with myself that morning. In my delirious state, I thought that maybe, with enough hope, Drew would miraculously reemerge, that with enough optimism he would stroll through the door as if none of it had ever happened. But my phone's cold glass stared back at me, a soulless reflection warping my tired face and distorting the tears streaking down my cheeks. I lifted the phone again, navigating to my text thread with Drew.

Please call, I typed.

My mind drifted back to hazy images of Mom, soaked with sweat on the starchy pillows of her hospital bed. I could still smell the disinfectant. Waiting for death felt easier back then. Maybe being a kid had protected me from the rawest edges of grief, my innocence like a shield. Or maybe the drawn-out nature of her sickness had made the burn slower, more bearable. Regardless, it stung more this time. We were supposed to end our night, stroll out the front door of the club, and pile into the back seat of an Uber. We were supposed to bury ourselves under a mound of McDonald's and giggle ourselves to sleep in front of a cheesy Netflix movie. We were supposed to wake up, hair disheveled, frantically searching for Advil. They were supposed to come home.

My phone buzzed, lurching me from delirium. No reply from Drew.

Few of us prepare for the task of delivering life-altering news to someone else's family. In war movies, a clean-shaven man in a neatly pressed uniform stoically strides up a walkway with his partner and taps on the front door. It creaks open slowly. He takes off his hat, dramatic music crescendos, and a heartbroken silhouette collapses in agony. Even though we know what's coming next, it's awful to watch, partly because the man's responsibility is nearly incomprehensible. How do you find the words to tell people that a loved one isn't coming home? How long do you hug them? How do you go to sleep that night, knowing they're curled up under heavy blankets, tears falling in the dark as they cry out for someone who can no longer hear them? It's a hellish task, and one I never thought I would need to be ready for.

I picked up the phone and began dialing the number I'd gotten from a Facebook message, my stomach a flurry of anxious energy. My finger hovered over the final digit. Making this phone call would mean it was real. No more hope that it might be a nightmare from which we would all awake. No more defiant denial. Just the harsh glare of reality. I don't remember hearing the line ring before a shaky voice greeted me. Juan's sister.

"Hi, this is his sister," she stammered. "What do you know? Please tell me he wasn't there."

I sat in stunned silence. In my haste to call her, I hadn't stopped to think about what I would say when she answered. She sounded younger than I had imagined, which only made it harder to find the right words. I pictured her sitting at the kitchen table, legs crossed tightly beneath her, clutching the phone. Would she have me on speaker for the entire family to hear? Or would she be alone, just the ticking of a nearby clock and the thud of her own heartbeat in her ears? She must have heard my nervous gulp because she pressed on.

"Please, Brandon. Please tell me he wasn't there. Please."

A single tear rolled slowly down my cheek. I wanted to hang up. To hug her. To scream angrily that none of this was fair. To vomit. *Of course he was there,* I thought. *It was supposed to be the safest space for us.* I opened my trembling lips and forced out the first words I could think of.

"I'm so sorry," I blurted. Nothing hopeful or eloquent. Just a vague, clumsy apology.

Parts of what happened in the summer of 2016 still haunt me when I close my eyes at night. I can't shake the image of the cup on the edge of the sink, beads of perspiration racing down its sides toward the cold porcelain bowl. Random nightmares, punctuated by the rancid stench of death that hung in the building that night, carry the scent of smoke and blood wafting by my nose as I drift off to sleep. The stunned looks of others who made it out, their clothes shredded and stained with blood, are burned into my subconscious. And I will never forget the scream of a mother who learned that the worst had happened to her child, the guttural howl of a heart shattering into dozens of tiny fragments.

Juan was an immensely proud person. He beamed when talking about the latest exam he had aced or the paper he had knocked out of the park. His joy nearly erupted through him when he bragged about a surprise he had picked up for Drew on his way home from the gym. And he brimmed with happiness when he talked about his family. He would launch headfirst into a story about game night at his sister's house, giggling about the cocktails they had mixed or boasting about the people he was most proud of. His sister. Her kids. His mother. Nothing thrilled Juan more than talking about his mother. He was the youngest of her children, the last to leave the nest. He was also a mama's boy, eager to brag about her and always willing to step out to answer her calls. She lovingly called him *el bebé*. Juan was proud to be her son, and she seemed immensely proud to love him. This deep well of affection now fueled her heartbroken screams.

Juan's sister sobbed softly on the other end of the line as his mother wailed in the background, her haunting cries sending shivers up my spine. I felt like an invader, listening in as a piece of her died alongside her child. I choked back my own tears, intent on being strong for them.

"I don't know where he is," I finally managed to explain. "I just know he was last seen getting into an ambulance, and now you have to go and find him."

~

I've always found the world to be—loud. Very loud. Even before I understood why, I sought out quiet as a form of recharge. The wail of a distant siren forces me to close all the windows in my apartment.

Chatter from the next table at a coffee shop prompts me to pick up my computer and work elsewhere. The buzz of a notification wakes me out of a dead sleep. But the deafening nature of the world around me goes beyond literal volume. Everything about the world is loud. Colors. Textures. Emotions. Each point in time is like an individual instrument in a cacophony of sound, carefully dancing around one another with the occasional explosive collision. A peaceful picnic in the park whispers softly, its quiet steadiness in harmony with the swaying grass and rustling tree limbs. Saying "I love you" for the first time trills anxiously in sync with a thudding heartbeat. Maybe that sensitivity to stimuli made the muted numbness of waiting for news so disorienting. A world once unrelentingly loud and raucous had suddenly and unexpectedly hushed. The birds seemed to stop chirping. The water in the pool outside was still and calm. No wind moved through the trees. Every word was murmured, every passing car muffled, as if the whole world were holding its breath, clinging to the frayed hope that no news was good news.

My phone buzzed from an incoming call, and I scrambled to dig it out from under a couch cushion. Juan's sister. Our conversation was brief and hurried, a mutual acknowledgment that anything more threatened to plunge us into an emotional void we wouldn't escape. Juan was dead. Gunshot wounds to multiple parts of his body. His lifeless figure was identified on an operating table, long after doctors had given up trying to save him. I had known sorrow, buffered by a child's inability to fully process it, but up until that point, I had thought heartbreak was just a tired cliché, a cinematic device used by rom-com directors to weave the same old theme through new characters and a fresh story line. Boy meets girl. Girl falls in love. Boy cheats. Heartbreak. They find resolution. The end. Until that brief call on the dirty stoop of my apartment, the door closed behind me so no one would have to watch me cry, heartbreak had only ever been a concept, an abstract diagnosis from a self-help series for which I'd be charged $14.99 for the paperback solution. But as I hung up and the phone slid from my shaking hand to the concrete below, I felt real heartbreak for the first time.

I buried my face in my hands and let out a scream, releasing the horror and fury I had been bottling up since the early hours of the morning. How could this be happening to me? To us? How would I find the words to tell the crowd waiting on the other side of the door, undoubtedly with more than a few ears pressed to it, hoping to catch a sliver of news? How would I tell Drew? How could I bring myself to grasp his hand, nudge him awake from a deep sleep, and crush what little hope he might have left? Heartbreak wasn't a concept—it was a hellscape. A bullet fragment, fresh from tearing at the fabric of everything I loved, sitting in a pool of blood next to Juan's lifeless body. A cage closing around my lungs, threatening to suffocate me with despair. I stood up and walked to a chair by the pool, thinking of plunging into the water and never coming up.

I never had to have that conversation with Drew. We got a call from his mother Monday morning. He had never made it off the dance floor. His body lay riddled with bullets in the dark recesses of Pulse—our refuge—decaying in the muggy Florida heat. I tried to muster the strength to scream, but all that came out was a whimper. My eyes were swollen and raw from an endless stream of tears, but I felt nothing. Numbness consumed me. And despite a steady crowd of friends and family members huddled around my coffee table, I was alone and empty. The world moved around me like a hurricane while I sat trapped in its eye, staring blankly at the swirling winds.

~

I loathed the prospect of moving from the couch. A haphazard stack of empty frozen dinner boxes had piled up on the hardwood next to me, the TV paused on an image of flashing police lights in front of the club. Outside, friends murmured anxiously. Drew had been announced dead by officers a few hours before, but somehow it already felt like a lifetime ago. I stared absently at the grainy image on the screen.

If I sit here long enough, maybe I'll wake up.

The front door creaked open, and a few tired friends piled in. They were speaking in hushed tones, still stunned by the shock of the last thirty-six hours. Part of me wanted them all to go away and let the silence envelop me for a while. But I was also deeply afraid of being alone, afraid that if I dozed off for too long, I would be instantly confronted by the glassy eyes of forty-nine lifeless bodies. I worried that more bad news might come. That I would finally collapse under the weight of it, with no one there to hold me up. That the darkness might consume me, might tempt me to pull a knife from the kitchen drawer and drag it across my wrists until everything went black. Although I badly wanted silence, I knew that being alone with my thoughts might end in disaster, so I was grateful for the company.

I eventually dozed off, my head dropping to the armrest as I stole a shred of relief after a sleepless night. The nightmares began almost immediately, with vivid intensity. I was in the damp bathroom of the club again, my back pressed against the concrete wall. Liquid pooled underneath me, the puddles again soaking the cuffs of my jeans. The plastic cup was exactly where I first saw it: perched on the edge of the sink. The smell of death hung heavy, practically smothering me. Behind me, a girl peed herself in terror, the warm liquid racing across the tiles in my direction. Everything was almost exactly as I remembered it. The hues of the poster on the walls, its corner curling in the humidity. The whimpers of the others trapped with me, trembling and clutching their knees. But something was off this time. The sound was different, more pronounced. The muffled roar of gunfire was replaced by the loud pops of an assault weapon just around the corner. The shooter had changed direction and was headed straight for us.

BANG BANG BANG BANG

The gunshots were interrupted by the sound of his boots crunching shards of broken glass. The footsteps drew closer.

BANG BANG BANG

Another girl let out a yelp behind me, a piece of glass jutting from the hand she had placed on the ground to steady herself. I frantically motioned for her to be quiet, but it was too late. Her shouting alerted the shooter, the pace of his boots accelerating.

BANG BANG

A shadowy figure rounded the corner and towered over us. I couldn't make out many details, but he wore a long black trench coat and a pair of black cargo pants. A jagged hunting knife hung from his utility belt. He cackled menacingly and raised the barrel of his assault rifle to my forehead, his finger toying with the trigger. I peered up, trying to paint a clearer picture of his sharp jawline and sloping forehead. Glossy black marbles stared back, opaque and unblinking. I opened my mouth to beg him to stop, but he let out a howl and squeezed the trigger.

BANG

I jolted awake with a scream. Just a dream.

A hand gently shook my shoulder. A friend stood over me, concern and pity on her face. "Sorry to wake you," she said. "But there's a vigil tonight, and I think it might be good for all of us to go."

My initial reaction was to scream "Hell no!" and lay my head back down. But I was afraid of who might be lurking behind my eyelids. And the idea of getting out of that tomb of an apartment sounded nice. The air inside was stagnant, and a cloud of gloom hung over everyone. Maybe being outside was what we needed. More than that, maybe seeing us was what the rest of the community needed. Up to then, we had been holed away in our makeshift command center, our only contact with the rest of the world via text messages and Facebook. I reluctantly agreed to go on one condition: we stick together.

~

I grabbed my already wilting bouquet of flowers and joined the group crossing the street toward the expansive lawn in front of the Dr. Phillips Center for the Performing Arts in downtown Orlando. The three-acre lawn ran the length of multiple city blocks and was teeming with people. Thousands had already gathered, embracing and crying. A friend spotted me in the crosswalk and sprinted toward me, dropping the bag he had brought and pulling me into a tight hug. I was masking my nervousness fairly well, though I had underestimated how overwhelmed I would be by large crowds, and I didn't want to lose my composure and embarrass myself. I hoped my friends would follow me if I made a mad dash for the car midway through the program.

It was comforting to see familiar faces and be in the company of others carrying a pain similar to mine. I had been so consumed by my own shock and grief that I hadn't had time to process the gravity of what had happened. I knew the death toll, of course, and I was aware of the international outpouring of support. But it was another thing to come face-to-face with the magnitude of it all, to stare down the sea of people grieving their own losses. I wondered how many of them knew Drew and Juan, how many would be crying for my best friends that night.

We slowly snaked our way through the crowd, stopping for hugs and words of empathy, until we reached the far side of the stage. The sun had already dipped below the horizon, making the heat more bearable. My gray polo shirt was dotted with sweat, but I was too dazed and exhausted to care. The stage was directly in front of us, its backdrop lit with brilliant rainbow lights. Throughout the night, speakers and artists paraded onto it to deliver somber words or sing haunting melodies. The mayor gave an address, underscoring the unity that had already bound us together in the hours since the shooting. The Orlando Gay Chorus sang beautiful, uplifting songs about love and healing. I wanted to hum along, or at least find some solace in their harmonies, but I could hardly hear them over the ringing in my ears and the numbness in my mind.

Friends behind me clutched one another, crying softly. Eric, inconsolable, wailed and wailed, crying out for those who had been stolen from us. I stared vacantly ahead, my heart a bottomless pit. I wasn't thinking about the crash of gunfire still reverberating in the back of my brain. I wasn't thinking about the tremble in my hands that had yet to subside. I wasn't thinking about Drew. I wasn't thinking about Juan. I just stared at the lectern, wondering when the hell we were supposed to wake up from this nightmare.

The choir sang a sweet, vaguely familiar tune as a group of people began passing out short white candles, each with an improvised paper handle to catch the wax. I held mine close to my chest, my hands still shaking. I took in the mass of people stretching in every direction. There was a spiritual presence in that place. I could feel the energy of everyone there, like a low thrum coursing between our bodies. I could feel Drew and Juan there, too, echoes of their tandem energies enveloping me. It struck me that this was as at home as I'd ever felt. Sure, we didn't meet the definition of a traditional family. And its most important members had just been stolen from us. But this outpouring of unconditional love was what I'd been searching for since I had first stuffed a few pairs of underwear into a suitcase and bounded down the jetway for a one-way trip to Orlando. Eight years after the journey had begun, I realized that I couldn't imagine living anywhere else. And I was more grateful for this community than I could put into words.

I focused on the dancing flame of my candle, fragile and fleeting, and I couldn't help but think of the forty-nine people we were there to mourn, each a flame of their own, beautiful and brilliant while they were here, then suddenly dark, cold, snuffed out. They deserved to see what a remarkable and resilient coalition they had unknowingly forged. They deserved to be there.

One by one, people lifted their candles toward the sky. A hush fell over the crowd. As if in a quiet act of solidarity, the entire world seemed to stop breathing. In the distance, a church bell chimed. One slow ring for each life taken too soon. I wanted to cry. I wanted to scream. I wanted to rush onstage and shout that none of this was fair. I wanted to shake myself in the hopes that when the world finally stopped spinning, I would still be lying by the pool with a half-empty drink melting in the sun beside me. I wanted it all to be a dream. But the ache in my heart remained. No sound escaped past the knot firmly rooted in my throat. I was furious and heartbroken—empty.

Much to my relief, the ceremony began to wind to a close. Reporters waited, so our group linked arms and began heading for a different exit to avoid them. I kept my head up, nodding and saying hello to friends and neighbors as we passed. Most looked exhausted, the horrors of the last thirty-six hours written on their faces. Many seemed relieved that the massive vigil and the agonizing wait for victims' names were behind them.

As we walked, my foot snagged on something, nearly tipping me over into the grass. I glanced down, trying to dislodge whatever it was. I bent down to inspect it: a photograph mounted on a wooden post. Drew's and Juan's faces exactly as they had been only days before. We had unknowingly stumbled across a makeshift memorial stretching across the middle of the lawn. Hundreds of mementos had been arranged there, collages and trinkets scattered among bursting bouquets of flowers. Families crouched by the images of their stolen loved ones, weeping into their hands and crying out angrily to God.

All at once, the strength I had mustered to brave the crowd was gone. My heart shattered all over again. There they were. Unchanged. As happy as I had left them, just hours before. As carefree as I had last seen them, twirling gleefully in each other's arms. The photo was one they had taken at SeaWorld, and they'd posted it just hours before the shooting, oblivious to what was coming. I wanted to call out to them and tell them to stay home. I wanted to beg them to ignore my message and crawl into bed early that night. I wailed, the pain radiating from deep inside me. But their smiles remained static. Frozen in time. The last remnants of who they were, reduced to flimsy photo paper.

I sank to my knees. The tears that I thought had run dry burst forth again, staining my thin gray polo. There was no holding back anymore. My chest heaved with pain. Every ounce of rage and exhaustion exploded from me, my shrieks bouncing off the glass panels of a nearby awning and echoing down the block. Embarrassed, I buried my face in my hands. No one was judging me for my grief, but somehow I still felt ashamed. As I knelt, blades of grass tickling my nose, my tears streaming, a pair of strong arms enveloped me, shielding me from the prying cameras. My consoler said nothing, silently holding me, rocking me back and forth while I cried. Whoever it was smelled faintly of cinnamon and cloves.

Time stood still. I don't know if we knelt for seconds, minutes, or hours. I wondered if it was another survivor or the family member of a victim. Regardless, I was grateful for the silent reminder of our collective commitment to care for one another, and for the emotional release, the first I had allowed myself.

My shoulders finished heaving, and my tears began to dry. I lifted my head to offer my thanks and looked into the face of a stranger. It was warm and understanding, dashes of golden brown powdered onto the brow. Her intense gaze was strong and steady. She wore a hijab, its soft burgundy fabric folded around her neck and tucked into the collar of her shirt. She put her hands on my shoulders, squeezed them tightly, and whispered, "Please know that you are loved."

I nodded gratefully, in awe of her selflessness. "Thank you," I said, wiping a stray tear from my chin. "You don't know how much I needed that."

~

President Barack Obama came to pay his respects and meet with us. I wish I had been composed enough to demand policy change or implore him to help us recover. I wish I'd had the forethought to consider what I would tell him in the fleeting time we had together. But I didn't. I lost my composure as soon as he reached out and took my hand. I buried my face in the shoulder of his pressed navy suit, blubbering into the soft, brushed fabric. His hug was firm and consoling. His shirt smelled faintly of cologne. Someone joked that he could be my father, and I chuckled, the first time I can remember laughing that week. Dignitaries came and went. Flowers piled up outside Drew's front door. The media stalked and hounded anyone willing to strap on a microphone and perform their trauma for a worldwide audience. I got in the car to go claim the credit card I had left open at the bar, only to turn around and head home when I caught wind that reporters were camped out in front of the building. My only respite was barricading myself in the bathroom, pretending to wash my hands for way too long so that I could try to stop the spinning in my skull.

The steady stream of loved ones through my apartment continued, their worried glances betraying fears that I might drown myself in the uncorked bottle of bourbon next to the bed. A few tried to lift my spirits, clumsily fumbling through small talk or showering me with words of affirmation.

"I'm so glad you're still here," a friend exclaimed nervously, washing the dishes I couldn't bring myself to tend to.

He was trying to make me feel better, but a wave of anger washed over me. "I'm not," I shot back, grinding the conversation to an awkward halt.

I didn't know how to feel about having escaped the club. The world wouldn't slow down long enough for me to process much of anything. But amid the blur of news cameras, candlelight vigils, stiff politicians in well-tailored suits, awkward embraces with vaguely familiar acquaintances, and throngs of people offering wine and pizza, one clear question hung over me: Did I deserve to die? After all, this is what people *like me* are supposed to go through, isn't it? When I was called a faggot at school, it was my fault for acting just a little too gay, for forgetting to stiffen my wrists or tone down my energy. If I tested positive for HIV, it would be my fault for being a "sexual deviant," the unavoidable consequence of not being strong enough to resist my urges. If I had come face-to-face with a gunman in a foggy nightclub, it was my fault for being there in the first place. For daring to dance unapologetically. For being selfish enough to want a place free of heteronormative chains, where boys kiss boys and no one gives a damn. Drew and Juan were better than I was. They were the best of all of us, their infectious optimism challenging everyone to see the good in one another. Yet their lights had been extinguished by a hateful man with a vendetta and hundreds of rounds of ammunition. Wasn't I supposed to die with them?

Tap tap tap

"Yeah, yeah," I growled. "Just a second."

I twisted the knobs on the bathroom faucet. I'd have plenty of time for these questions later.

~

There's nothing easy about planning a funeral service you aren't prepared for, and it's exponentially harder inside the pressure cooker of public interest. A group of us gathered in Drew's dimly lit living room. His landlord was gracious enough to let us use the apartment for a few weeks. Feeling close to Drew while we discussed how to best memorialize him somehow made it hurt a little less. I curled up in my usual chair, its leather worn and soft. It was oversize, allowing me to tuck my legs underneath myself and sink into its sagging cushion. Everything about the place still smelled like him. A clean, masculine warmth that, if I imagined hard enough, made everything feel normal for an instant.

Drew was the social glue at the intersection of more than a few groups of friends. He had acted as a bridge between the gay boys who seemed to live under a set of free weights at LA Fitness and those of us too skinny to keep our pants up without a belt. He moved effortlessly between the Instagram-ready beauties and the rest of us, a hodgepodge of average people with nothing in common except him. He brought us all together, forced us to push past our own egos and get to know someone new. Everyone claimed him as a best friend, which meant that the most important task we faced was choosing a funeral space big enough for everyone. We scoured the city in search of a perfect location, and eventually his mother landed on a beautiful cathedral downtown, a stunning historic building with rows and rows of polished pews.

We got to the church long before others, and we were ushered through a back door onto the grounds. A beautiful courtyard was dotted with flowers, its calm greenery a respite from downtown's bustling chaos. It was quiet but not the eerie, unsettling silence of my apartment. This place was peaceful. I could sense Drew in it. I let out a quiet sigh and allowed my shoulders to relax a little.

At one end of the long walkway, we mounted a narrow staircase. Despite the calming tranquility of the church garden, I still couldn't shake a deep feeling of numbness. Emptiness. I knew the flowers speckling the grass below were beautiful, but to me they appeared muted. Graying stems with faded petals. The sky was dull and flat, its brilliant blue lost on me. Chirping birds sounded miles away, their trills drowned out and inaudible. I didn't feel resentment. Or sadness. I couldn't feel joy or summon laughter. A hollow void loomed where a thunderous roar of emotions had stirred before. I wished we didn't have to be there at all.

I touched the breast pocket of my blazer with one hand to make sure that the tightly folded papers were still there. I'd been assigned several tasks for the service, one being to deliver a brief eulogy. I was both honored and a nervous wreck. How do you capture the most beautiful person you've ever known in the time between commercial breaks on local television coverage of his funeral service? How do you tell people what he meant to you without dissolving into a barrage of screams? I had scribbled down my words a few hours earlier in the front seat of my car. I write best in total silence, when my thoughts aren't obstructed by the murmur of the world around me. Armed with a Red Bull, I tried to put Drew's spirit onto paper. I would write a few lines, then strike them furiously before crumpling the page and tossing it angrily onto the passenger seat.

Drew was the best person I ever—
Cross out, crumple, toss.
One time, Drew and I went—
Definitely not that. Cross out, crumple, toss.

I decided to work more slowly, stopping every few strokes to steady my quivering hand. I told myself not to overthink it, just to write what I felt. I scratched a few words and paused to read it.

We all have those once-in-a-lifetime people.

That one. That's Drew.

My other role that day was to serve as a pallbearer. I didn't think much of it when Drew's mom asked me. I wasn't terribly familiar with funerals but had seen the word in books and was willing to do anything to make the service special. The priest led us down another narrow staircase, and each step creaked as we tiptoed down. I imagined all the devastated families who had crept down those stairs before, hundreds of years of grieving congregants descending into the cathedral to bid final farewells to friends and family members gone too soon. I wondered if they, too, had felt hollow voids in their hearts or watched the color fade from tulips in the garden. I wondered if they had found the strength to write a eulogy and whether their hands had trembled too. We filed to the foyer to take our places next to the casket.

I was stunned when the doors to the nave opened. We had discussed the possibility of his friends and family arriving *en masse*, but there wasn't an empty seat in the cathedral. Every row was packed with pressed suits and crisp black dresses. Friends from previous stages of Drew's life crowded in the back of the great hall, leaning on one another's shoulders and swaying gently to the hypnotic melody of an organ. Over a thousand people crammed into the cathedral that day, spilling out of the foyer and into the streets. And I recognized every face. The neighbor who saw us at our best. The bartender who saw us at our worst. Drew had brought us all together—one last time.

The coffin lurched forward, and the haunting sounds of the organ grew with every step. Drew's casket was beautiful, a welcome distraction from the aggressive stares of family and friends. The polished wood gleamed, proud and regal. A stunning pall was draped across the top, its intricate gold design cut by a deep-red cross that spanned from one end to the other. Unlike the flowers in the courtyard, this was vibrant and vivid. The tan wood glowed, as if the warmth of Drew's energy radiated from inside. As we trudged forward, my grip on the pall got tighter and tighter. I traced the woven details with the pads of my fingers to calm my nerves and stop the sobs brewing just beneath the surface of my composure. In some ways, it felt as if Drew were walking alongside me, one gangly arm draped over my shoulders while he beamed from ear to ear. And in others, it was a stark reminder that he was gone. I crumpled an edge of the fabric in my fist and choked back a few tears.

We reached the front of the congregation and stopped. The brightly lit altar was adorned with colorful rugs and tall wooden sculptures. Those of us who loved Drew would eventually file up to the pulpit and try to make sense of it all. In the center of the stage was a long table draped in white cloth, set for a Communion service. And illuminated above it all hung a towering Jesus, a huge stone figure on a wooden cross. I hated churches. Sweat began to bead on my forehead, and I wondered silently if God could hear my thoughts. Couldn't hurt to find out.

How could you let this happen to us?

How can you sit up there and watch people suffer without batting an eye?

Why did they have to die?

I hate you.

I inhaled sharply, recoiling from my own dark thoughts and glancing up at the mammoth statue suspended above the stage, half expecting it to spout flames and devour me. It stared back blankly, unflinching.

Figures you wouldn't hear me.

The priest motioned us toward a pew in the front. My heart rate accelerated, and I laid a hand on the burnished wooden casket. I couldn't let go yet. I hadn't found the right words to say goodbye. My mind raced back to a week earlier. Drew's arm draped over my shoulders. Stars shimmering above our heads. Muggy air perforated by the buzz of insects in a nearby palm tree. Things had been easy then. Life had been easy. I wished I'd taken the time to cherish it. I wished I'd spent more time appreciating what I had instead of clawing greedily for more. I wished I hadn't been too caught up in the mundane—rush-hour traffic, parking tickets, failed first dates—to see what was right in front of me.

Drew taught me to love myself. He showed me what was possible when I was unashamed and unapologetic. He had shrugged off the suggestion that the world wasn't ready for us and defiantly demanded that it be. Because of Drew, I was, for perhaps the first time, proud to be me.

A single tear trickled down my cheek and fell silently.

Proud. That's the word I was searching for. Drew had made me proud. I leaned toward the casket and whispered my final goodbye.

"I will never stop fighting for a world you would be proud of."

CHAPTER 7

POWER IN PURPOSE

I didn't decide to write a book out of some bloated sense of ego or as a vanity project. In fact, the entire process has been fraught with impostor syndrome and marked by late nights wondering who on earth will even crack the cover once it's all said and done. I've lost sleep over how people will perceive the words I've written about them and considered changing my name and buying a one-way plane ticket to Mykonos so that my publisher can't find me. Writing is challenging. If anyone thinks they're going to casually plop down and pen a memoir as one long pat on their own back, or to punch a ticket toward fame and riches, they should think again. In truth, this book was born from a deep sense of obligation—of purpose.

I made the decision to begin chronicling my experiences in the summer of 2020. On May 25, outside a convenience store in Minneapolis, George Floyd was murdered by white police officer Derek Chauvin. The brutal video was widely shared across social media. For over nine excruciating minutes, Chauvin asphyxiated Floyd, whose desperate pleas for his mother and cries of "I can't breathe" shocked the world and ignited the largest civil rights protests in our nation's history. It was sickening to anyone with a conscience, and yet just another example of the thumb under which Black people in America live every day. The plotline is a tired one. Very real anger at pervasive police violence and systemic racism against Black people is ignored until it is caught on camera and force-fed to those shielded by white privilege ad nauseum. A clamor for justice ensues from those who hadn't been paying attention. Politicians make promises. Television producers create content. It feels as though change is finally coming. But it's not. Eventually, the pressure fades, a new headline takes over, and the harsh glare of the television cameras goes dark, leaving Black people screaming into the void until the next brutalized body makes prime-time coverage.

I was mad. Infuriated that this could happen to someone in broad daylight in the twenty-first century. Enraged by media coverage that reduced the life of a man—a father, a son—to points on a partisan scoreboard. Heartbroken for a family forced to eat around a table with an empty seat. But there was another emotion lurking under the righteous ire that fueled my feet as I marched with my clenched fist in the air. I felt guilty. I didn't understand why I felt guilty, just that I did. And with that guilt came shame. I peered from one masked face to the next at a protest, feverishly searching for anyone who had clocked that I didn't belong. I lost sleep worrying over the absurd idea that I had somehow played a role in George Floyd's demise. I couldn't explain it. Until I got a call from my boss, Nadine.

She had taken note of the hollowness in my voice during that week's staff call. I've never been very good at hiding my emotions on a Zoom screen, a trait that is as much a hindrance as an asset, and the added weight of the events in Minneapolis that week made my attempt to do so futile. When Nadine called to follow up with me, she wasted no time.

"You seem closed off," she said crisply. "How are you feeling?"

I fumbled through a nonanswer about how the murder was fueling my resolve to work harder. That part was true. George Floyd's killing really did serve as a reminder of everything at stake in our work. In 2019, I had given up a burgeoning career in Starbucks management to jump into full-time advocacy. At the time I had no idea what that would entail, but I knew I could no longer just sit on the sidelines, staring at spreadsheets filled with profits and losses. I had seen the potential to effect change and, try as I might, couldn't unsee it. I wanted to force the world to hear our stories, and I knew that I needed the power of an organization behind me. I wanted to learn the ugly details of how policy is made so that I could wield this knowledge—and the power that comes with it—as a tool against an unjust system. I was still messy, my grief not always neatly packaged and my approach to advocacy sometimes abrupt. I would break down midspeech in an unexpected cascade of emotions. But Nadine took a chance on me. I logged off my corporate-issued laptop, signed out of my Starbucks.com email account, and joined the team at Equality Florida, the statewide LGBTQ+ civil rights organization led by Nadine, herself a Black lesbian, and her colleagues.

It didn't take long for me to see how intertwined all of our struggles are. Justice is justice. And the denial of justice for any one group of people erodes justice for all people. Attacks on the rights of transgender people to access health care are tied to assaults on abortion rights, as both are grounded in a fight for sexual autonomy, a tug-of-war with the government over control of our own bodies. The fight for immigrant rights is an LGBTQ+ fight, too, because it is a collective demand for human-centered politics that treat people with a basic level of decency. And the work of dismantling systemic racism is ours as well. The queer community includes people of color. And when the state is empowered to defend white supremacy, violently and brutally, all of our lives are on the line. To paraphrase Fannie Lou Hamer, Dr. Martin Luther King Jr., and Maya Angelou: so long as a single person has not been liberated, none of us has truly been liberated. What I told Nadine wasn't entirely a lie. I did feel a renewed sense of obligation to our fight. But I was still masking the truth.

"I'm not asking about the work," she pressed. "I'm asking how you feel."

"Guilty," I blurted out. "And I don't know why."

We sat on the phone for nearly half an hour, diagnosing the root of my shame. I tried to articulate what I was experiencing while Nadine listened quietly on the other end. I told her that despite feeling the same communal indignation at injustice that everyone else did, there was a disorienting sense of disconnect between me and the pained Black faces marching in the streets. I could see their silhouettes and hear their cries, but I couldn't quite make out the words. I felt a profound dread that I didn't know what it really felt like to be Black in America, that when my own community spoke out, I didn't know the words with which to reply. I stammered about my fear that, in some twisted way, I had contributed to the conditions leading to George Floyd's murder. I confessed that, as part of my desperate attempt to survive being a queer Black kid in a threatening white community, my assimilation may have severed my ties to others like me. I told her that, in an effort to stay alive, I might have unwittingly divorced myself from half of who I am. And for that, I felt profoundly ashamed.

I paused, embarrassed. I had never admitted any of these things out loud, let alone described this debilitating loss of identity to someone at work.

Nadine's voice was steady, unwavering. "I hope you understand that none of that is your fault. It is a function of oppression to decouple us from the power of our collective."

I was quiet. No one had so effortlessly encapsulated the weight that I carried every day, the shame with which I showed up in far too many spaces. I was transported back to moments when I had been forced as a kid to swallow the racism around me in order to survive. Times I was told to watch my wallet when visiting cousins. Times I heard adults yelling at immigrants to speak English and buried my intense revulsion. The countless dinner conversations about needing to be the exception to the rule if I wanted to amount to anything. All of it while my only frame of reference at the time drove a wider and wider wedge between me and the people now sobbing for justice on the streets. That dissociation from my own identity, foisted on me by figures of authority, had by design chiseled me off from an entire community, leaving me like a fractured pebble in the middle of a desolate highway, tumbling aimlessly and alone. My guilt was replaced by a renewed fury against this self-serving system of divide and conquer—and a sense of determination to expose it for what it is.

So I decided to write it down. All of it. I committed to braving the ugliest parts of what I've seen and sharing the unvarnished truth, no matter who might be shocked. Because I understood that this new revelation came with a heavy responsibility, an obligation to tell the next generation of mixed-race kids that there is infinite power in who they are. More than that, I wanted to tell them how I survived. Survived a deadly terrorist attack. Survived the unimaginable pain of losing my people. Survived the perils of childhood without my greatest champion. Survived the traps set for me by a world that has for so long sought to diminish and extinguish people like us. I felt like I owed it to them to explain how I got here, and to commit publicly to making good on my promise to Drew. I took my guilt, faced it head-on, and turned it into the most powerful antidote to despair that I've discovered: purpose.

Community has saved my life more than once. They didn't know it, but the cheerful faces of my Starbucks customers kept me alive after that night at Ben's apartment, the singsong tones in their morning greetings dulling the sharp edges of my ache. The new friends I had made in Orlando gave me a reason to believe in myself after years of spiraling deeper and deeper into self-loathing. The entire city rallied around me after the shooting, keeping me from falling off the precipice of grief into oblivion. But if community saved my life, it was purpose that set me free.

When you lose someone you love most, you fly through a vast chasm of emotions. Deep sorrow fuels an endless stream of tears. Intense rage washes over you. You pound a plush sofa cushion with clenched fists and bury your face in a pillow. You flash back to an inside joke, pick up your phone, and remember that no one will answer. I first felt all of these emotions when Mom died. And I was mostly prepared for how to navigate them. I let them crash into me like waves on a rocky shore, content in the understanding that they would pass. But I wasn't ready for the fear. Fear of forgetting how Drew smelled prompted me to stash one of his favorite T-shirts in my top dresser drawer. Fear of forgetting Juan's voice incited a panicked sprint through my phone for old videos. I don't remember the day I realized that I no longer remembered the softness of my mother's skin, despite having nuzzled it countless times as a kid. I don't know if the hollow place where that memory once lived scares me or simply makes me sad. But I know that the fear of forgetting Drew and Juan was unshakable.

I was also deeply afraid that the world would never know them as I did. Drew changed my life. Juan made it more complete. Before them, I had been a lonely shell. I hadn't known what it meant to be unapologetic, unashamed, and proud. Whether they knew it or not, Drew and Juan taught me to put on my favorite outfit without succumbing to a wave of anxiety that I might look too gay. They pushed me to tear down my insecurities and greet a stranger at a bar. My friendship with Drew and Juan was the safest space I knew, a refuge from the harsh glare of the world outside. And I was terrified that to those only just tuning in, they would be little more than names etched on aging stone, their beauty trapped in a cold, hard slab of granite.

∼

A group crowded close together, gathering around the ottoman where the news anchor sat. No one knew the first thing about being on camera, but we had collectively established a few ground rules. First, we would speak only from the place where we felt most at home: Drew's apartment. If we were going to bare the most vulnerable parts of our souls, share the most gut-wrenching memories of the friends we had lost only hours before, we were going to do it from our usual spots. Second, our interview would focus on only the night of the shooting and the lives of Drew and Juan. Sensationalist headlines were already concentrating on the identity and lived experiences of the shooter. Rumors swirled on the internet about whether he was secretly gay. People had seen him at the club before the night of the shooting or sent him messages on Grindr. Others wondered aloud whether his wife should have done something to stop him. Islamophobic vitriol spewed from every corner of the coverage, forcing others to answer for the violence and hatred that only he was responsible for. The shooter's story wasn't important to us. It's still not important to me, which is why I refuse to use his name. The stories that merit telling are the ones about the people who deserve to be here, the stories whose endings were stolen.

I chose my favorite leather chair, and the rest crowded onto the couch and clutched hands. The camera crew scurried around, adjusting lights. I still couldn't stop the speed with which the world was whirling around me. I felt trapped, stuck in slow motion while the rest of the universe flew by like a freight train. The mood was somber and quiet as we shifted nervously in our seats and tried to hold back tears. We knew we would get only one shot at introducing the world to our little chosen family, and we felt enormous pressure to get it right. The anchor took her perch and pinned a microphone to the lapel of her jacket. I recognized her from CNN clips that I had seen online. I always thought she seemed stern and intimidating behind her desk in New York City, but sitting in front of us, she had a calming energy. She was pretty, with a disarming charm. Her wavy blond hair had been perfectly coiffed by a team of stylists. Her makeup was carefully painted. A little notepad sat near her crossed legs. She wore a khaki military jacket, and a pair of dark-rimmed glasses were perched near the tip of her nose. When she had situated herself and quietly reviewed her notes, she motioned toward the cameraman, looked up, and inhaled.

"I know it's hard, but . . . can you tell me about that night?"

We took turns recapping how the nightmare had unfolded for us. Voices wavered and cracked at first, but they gained strength. Most of the group had already gone to bed when the shooting happened, so their stories were similar. They slept without a care in the world, only to be awakened by the worst news imaginable. There was panic. Then fear. Then heartbreak. Now, numbness. Each of us was still stunned, unable to process the hell that had descended upon our little world.

I managed to maintain my composure for longer than I had expected, recounting the night with painstaking detail. The first sound of gunshots. The stench hovering in the air. Bone-chilling screams from the dark recesses of the club. My friends nodded encouragingly. Eventually, I arrived at the part of the story in which I escaped to safety while Drew and Juan lay trapped inside. I knew it was coming and had steeled myself to share it without coming unglued. But the image of them lying helpless, in pools of their own blood, their bodies perforated by a dozen rounds, was too much to bear. I wept, and my voice shook as I pressed on. By the end, I was little more than a puddle, my hand tightly clutching someone else's. The reporter listened quietly and patiently as we laid out the events that had led up to our sitting together, huddled in Drew's living room, face-to-face with TV cameras. She didn't rush us or grow annoyed when we needed to stop and reach for tissues. Instead, she nodded reassuringly and allowed us to talk at our own, jumbled pace.

When our voices finally trailed off, every painful detail of the previous days splayed out for all to see, the reporter adjusted her glasses and sighed lightly. "What can you tell me about Drew and Juan?"

A weight lifted. We'd have been forgiven for getting lost in the agony of how they were stolen from us, but her question was a reminder of why we had agreed to sit down for the interview in the first place: our unanimous agreement that we now had an obligation to preserve the legacies of our best friends. We practically tripped over one another to share our favorite stories. We laughed about old memories and let a worldwide audience in on a few inside jokes. Our stories about the night of the shooting varied wildly, but in recounting the lives that Drew and Juan had lived, we all trilled in perfect unison. They had been the best of us, the ones who had challenged us to be better every day. Even on the most mundane days, we had been lucky to have them. And the world needed to hear that. Drew and Juan didn't just matter because of the brutal way they were murdered; they mattered because of the beautiful ways they had lived. The love they had shared with us—and for each other—was worth shouting out loud. The community they had created, for anyone lucky enough to know them, was worth memorializing. Our plea to the country—the world—was to honor their stolen lives, but not by obsessing over a man with a history of dangerous and violent speech or over the generalized feuds between marginalized communities that were being manufactured in the media. Our plea was to celebrate—defiantly—the people who should still be with us and to ensure that their names and their stories lived on.

We wrapped up the interview, piles of crushed tissues scattered at our feet, and thanked the crew for agreeing to meet with us on our terms. They were humble and gracious, thanking us individually for being vulnerable and allowing them into our sacred space. They packed their gear quietly, taking care not to bump or disturb anything on their way out. The last to depart was the reporter, who had lingered just a little longer to share hugs and words of encouragement. She stepped outside the door and turned back one last time.

"Thank you for sharing your stories," she said. "They were beautiful souls, and this is just the beginning. May they be a catalyst for change."

The door closed behind her, and we exhaled.

When the interview aired, I felt hope for the first time since the shooting. All too often I had been a consumer of tragedies like ours. I would flip on the television while cooking and see the shards of some heartbroken community in a distant part of the country parading across the screen. I would turn up the volume, intrigued by the details, but like others, I would grow weary of the pain and change the channel, pushing the shared grief aside. Empathy is a heavy weight to carry when it feels like the whole world is teetering on the edge of apocalypse. And I didn't feel particularly guilty changing the channel, knowing that I was hardly the only one doing it. The public outcry never seemed to last much longer than a single news segment. Mass shootings are so common that most of them never rise to the news cycle at all. The country barely has time to learn the name of a city torn apart by gun violence before the next commercial break, and almost never gets a chance to learn the stories of those who were killed. But I felt hope, because this time could be different. This time, we could force the world to hear their names and consider their lives. This time, we could insist that we put a stop to all of it. We had taken the first step toward writing a new ending to this tragedy, and I just *knew* the world would have to listen.

But that hope was short lived. Our powerful segment was buried by competing headlines almost as soon as it aired. A processional of talking heads—mostly cisgender, heterosexual white men—appeared on every major network, weighing in on the worst night of our lives. They talked about Orlando at length. They discussed the "radical Islamic terrorism" at the root of the shooting, practically begging for xenophobia to be further baked into law. They rejected conversations about gun-safety reforms, casting those issues as unnecessarily political, even as they reduced our existence to pieces on a political chessboard. They talked about Donald Trump's narcissistic and obscene tweets in the aftermath of the shooting. They bemoaned Hillary Clinton's "performative" gestures of goodwill. Politicians put on makeup and leaped in front of any camera they could find, desperate to milk the opportunity for all possible PR benefits.

The coverage was wall to wall. No one in America could turn on a nightly news show without being bombarded by ready-made graphics and the concerned voices of cable TV anchors fretting over how forty-nine dead bodies in a nightclub might influence the outcome of the next election. They were talking about Orlando, but they weren't saying anything about *us*. The few segments that honored the lives of those murdered were almost immediately drowned out by sensationalist pearl clutching over how this might play with voters in rural Pennsylvania. As survivors lay clinging to life in hospital beds, their bodies ravaged by gaping exit wounds, commentators took turns in the spotlight to paint June 12 as just another bad day in the war on terror. It felt like we had poured our hearts out in vain. We had begged them to listen to our stories in the hope that this time could be different, but the tragedy porn churned on.

I waited a few days, hoping things would get better. Surely the appetite for fearmongering and naked partisanship would fade, and our stories would cut through. Surely some rational minds would see the grotesque nature of it all and pull us back from the abyss. But those hopes never materialized. Gay and bisexual men were turned away at blood-donation centers, denied the chance to help their communities because of decades-old bigotry embedded in Food and Drug Administration policy. Still, the media droned on. Resources poured in from around the globe, flooding the accounts of large LGBTQ+ organizations that were already flush with cash, while those who are often least served by these organizations—queer people of color, transgender people, immigrants—were ignored. Still, the media droned on. Undocumented family members of victims struggled with whether to come forward and ask for support out of fear that federal law enforcement, the gatekeepers to care, would deport them. Still, the media droned on.

Ten days after the shooting, failed presidential candidate Marco Rubio announced his intent to run for reelection to the US Senate, just one month after a snarky tweet writing off the idea. In his pathetic wordsmithing, he cited the attack on Pulse as a motivating factor in his decision. Never mind that he firmly opposed any policy changes that might have prevented what happened to us. Never mind that he had just completed an embarrassing sprint into the gutter of presidential politics, comparing dick sizes with Donald Trump on a debate stage through thinly veiled euphemisms. Like almost everyone else, Rubio chose to see an opening for himself rather than our humanity. An opportunity to amass more power. There we were, a community shredded by violence and relegated to the sidelines as malignant narcissists used our pain as their own political headwind. I was enraged. Infuriated. And determined to make them hear us.

I didn't set out to jump into the meat grinder of politics myself. I just wanted someone to know how angry I was. I sat down and opened my computer, the cursor blinking on the search bar. How could I make the biggest impact? Who would even bother to answer my call? I browsed the pages of a few local Democrat groups. Though well intentioned, they all seemed to lack the kind of reach I imagined we'd need in order to make a difference. Our community needed a louder microphone, a bigger stage. Up to that point, we had championed love and affirmation. And while those were still critical values to guide us, the world needed our fury too. It needed to see our faces and hear our voices, to be confronted by the failures of the same leaders who would jump to take advantage of us before we could even finish holding funerals for all of our friends. We needed to go right at those who saw our suffering as a chance to build their brands. Curious, I searched for Rubio's opponent. Patrick Murphy was a friendly-looking congressman with a fighting chance. He might be the right place to start. I clicked the "Contact Me" button and began to draft my note.

> I want to mobilize the city of Orlando and end Marco Rubio's career. How can I help?

Tragedies are unpredictable. The ripples they leave behind don't always hit when or where you expect them. They don't always wash over us with the same strength. Each one comes with its own unique signature. Sometimes I turn on the nightly news, listen to the story of yet another mass casualty event, and feel a normal sense of empathy. My heart still shatters for those impacted, but I'm not crushed under the weight of what's on my screen. Sometimes the stories of other communities plunged into the same vicious descent as mine serve as a sobering reminder of what's at stake. Other times, the headline cracks me.

I was at work when I got the first text messages. It had been a year since I had first packed my bags, taken a new position at Starbucks, and relocated to Tallahassee, in large part to escape the constant suffocating reminders of the shooting. An escapism that was now being shattered, one cell-phone vibration at a time.

Thinking about you. Let me know if you need to talk.

I hope you're not watching TV.

Hey, are you okay?

Not again.

By then, I had experienced enough of these situations to know what was happening. Another shooting. Another city trending. Another long list of names. It is America's unique shame that day after day, week after week, gun violence tears families apart while those in positions of power do nothing. And there are few things more American than entire generations of mass-shooting survivors learning to identify the signs that yet another community is under attack—our permanent gift from an apathetic government that doesn't care how many of its citizens are tortured by PTSD so long as nothing interrupts the cash flow or balance of power. I got up from the table, zipped my bag, and jogged out the front door of the Starbucks store I had been working in. It's always easier if I can glue myself to the news and process it on my own.

If some tragedies trigger a series of ripples, this one was a barrage, hitting all at once, like an unexpected tsunami on a sunny afternoon. The once quiet Florida suburb of Parkland had fallen victim to the same fate we had. The headline scrolled across the ticker at the bottom of the TV screen as I stared blankly, a familiar numbness forming in the pit of my stomach. Marjory Stoneman Douglas High School. Valentine's Day. Seventeen people shot and killed. The cheeks of their families and friends were stained with the same kind of tears that had dried on my own face just a few years before. Nothing would ever be the same there. Some would never sleep through the night again. Some would be forever traumatized, haunted by the empty seat at the dinner table. The entire city would be rocked by the attack, whole neighborhoods upended. My heart broke for every one of them. My anger simmered, fueled by a disbelief that we could call ourselves a "great nation" while standing idly by as entire communities were mowed down.

I couldn't pull myself away from this one. I placed a throw pillow under me on the hardwood floor and sat inches from the TV screen, mesmerized by the coverage. Tears rolled off my chin. These were not faces of people like me. They weren't adults. They were *children*, their fragile innocence stripped from them by brutal violence, their joy stolen away, their youthful glow snuffed out and replaced with the cold, hard reality of a world in which they were expendable. This one hurt more because I knew what these young people were going to suffer through. I knew the nightmares they would have, the cold sweats they would wake up from. I knew how frantically they would search for exits in grocery stores and how they would stare down strangers with oversize backpacks on the subway. I knew how strong they would try to be, saving their tears for the silence and solitude of their bedrooms, long after their parents had gone to sleep, only to crumble into fractured shells of who they used to be. My heart broke for them. They deserved better. We all do. But especially them. They deserved a world that fought to protect them and see them thrive, not a world that tossed them into the blaze of our darkest impulses and watched as they were devoured.

Less than a week later, a group of Parkland students planned a rally outside the state capitol to demand action from lawmakers on gun violence. They coordinated buses for the seven-hour trip to Tallahassee, arranged for meetings with elected officials, and organized a protest outside the capitol building. With wisdom beyond their years, they determined that the most effective strategy was to apply maximum pressure, both inside and outside, forcing state legislators to decide whether they would take action or sit silently as tens of thousands of fed up young people amassed.

In honor of the victims and those brave students, leaders in Tallahassee had planned a vigil for the night of their arrival. I hurried to the closet and slipped on a pair of jeans and an unattractive sweater. It had been a long day at work, and I was already running late, so I didn't have time to be picky. I tucked a few essentials into a bag and bounded down the steps of the porch to my car. Much of the initial shock had worn off, replaced by a familiar wave of exhaustion. Crises like these took everything out of me. The night terrors that I managed to hold at bay came roaring back, wreaking havoc on my sleep schedule. The relentless buzz of my phone, as reporters called for comment, was suffocating. And all of it against the backdrop of my sorrow for those kids whose lives had been turned upside down. I crawled into the front seat and started the engine.

For an instant, I considered going back inside. I could make some excuse for my absence—an unexpected work meeting or an emergency at home. I didn't know if I had the emotional bandwidth to congregate and mourn yet more gut-wrenching losses. Moving a few hundred miles away and taking a cushy promotion had been designed, in part, to separate me from reliving the hell of Pulse every day. I wanted to take a breath, to disconnect myself from the crushing weight of violence and death. But it was inescapable, and I wasn't sure how I would handle being in a space full of fresh wounds so like those that had only just begun to scar for me. I didn't know how I would respond when they were struck by my same sense of desperation, searching for some sort of meaning in the hopelessness.

I pulled out of the driveway. It was important for me to be there and selfish of me to center my own discomfort. The night wasn't about *me*. When I got to the venue, people had already begun gathering in a cavernous warehouse with cracked concrete floors and tall brick walls. The doors were propped open, so the attendees were bundled in sweaters and jackets, holding tightly to one another's arms. A bare, modest stage had been constructed on one side of the room. In front of it sat a makeshift memorial: flowers and candles carefully placed next to photos of those who had been murdered. Visitors paused in front of the polished frames, the haunting ghosts staring back, frozen in time behind thin layers of glass.

A steady stream of people began to file in—community leaders, friends, neighbors—offering hushed condolences to each other as they made their way toward the memorial. Frequent gusts of cold air pushed friends closer together. I was proud of how many had come to show their support. The last thing these courageous students needed was to be met by a lackluster show of apathy. I recognized more than a few people among the crowd and waved discreetly from my refuge in the back.

My anxiety was already high. There's something uniquely triggering about the imagery that follows a mass shooting: the iconic white wooden crosses painted with the names of victims, bundles of colorful flowers tucked under the corners of picture frames, battery-powered candles faintly flickering. My mind flooded with excruciating memories of the world gawking at our grief. In case I needed to dart out unexpectedly, I huddled at the edge of a group of onlookers near the door. I scanned the immense space, first identifying the exits, then noting the powerful people sprinkled throughout the crowd: state lawmakers, local elected officials, powerful community advocates who had been fighting to end gun violence and demilitarize hate for years. I wondered how many of them had grown exasperated. I thought about how many were willing to stand on well-lit stages and deliver rousing speeches but were nowhere to be found when it was time to do the real work. Still, I was grateful that so many had shown up in solidarity.

A hush descended over the building as a single-file line of students marched in. Against the backdrop of the tall brick walls, they were diminutive. Each pair of eyes was puffy and red. They clutched each other's arms, trembling. I was struck by how young they were, children forced to bear witness to more violence than most people will see in an entire lifetime. It weighed heavily on their slumped shoulders as they worked their way slowly to the front and gathered near the stage and its tiny pile of flowers. Some cried silently. Some wept aloud. Others stared without seeing, hollowed by their grief.

Hold it together, Brandon.

The speaking program came to a close. Everyone was still for a moment of silence in honor of the seventeen victims. A few students whimpered. A handful of their teachers sobbed softly in each other's arms. It was all so brutally familiar, like a sick nightmare relived. Their tears were our tears. Their horror was our horror. I was trying to maintain my composure and observe the moment of silence when a firm hand grabbed my arm and pulled me.

It was a friend, an elected leader I knew from Orlando. "You need to talk to these kids," he murmured.

My heart skipped a beat. I was already a blubbering mess. And I had no idea what to say to a group of teenagers publicly grieving the vicious murder of their peers. What could I offer that would bring them any solace? What words might numb the torment of having to attend a dozen funerals before you've gotten to ask someone to prom?

"I don't know what I would say," I whispered back, trying to steady my shallow breathing.

"I don't know what you'll say either. But you're the only one who knows what they're going through. They need to hear that it's going to be okay."

He nudged me in the direction of the students. They had shifted into a tight circle, shielding themselves from onlookers while they held each other and cried. I thought of the disorienting first vigil I had attended. People couldn't decide whether to approach us and share their condolences or give us space to grieve in peace, so they just gawked invasively. It felt like an out-of-body experience at the time, as if I were watching my own body stumble through the crowd, unable to process what was going on. Were these students feeling the same? They were fresh from an hours-long bus ride and days away from funerals they never could have expected. Almost overnight they had gone from studying for math tests to practicing speeches for national TV. And now here they stood, clumped like caged animals as a horrified community watched, unable to protect or heal them.

I inched closer, frantically thinking about what I would say. My friend's stare burned a pair of holes in the back of my neck. He wouldn't stop until I'd followed through. I wanted to offer advice, to be a source of hope, to strike a perfect balance between being understanding and realistic. I knew from experience that few things are more infuriating than patronizing, tone-deaf, unsolicited words of wisdom.

God never gives us more than we can handle.

Don't worry, it gets easier.

Stay strong.

I had heard these empty platitudes countless times after Drew and Juan were murdered, and they never stung any less. I wanted to give these students a reason to hope, to encourage them to lean on each other. I wanted to tell them all the things I had learned. I wanted them to know that they weren't alone, that even when the cameras clicked off and the world's attention faded, they would still have an ally in me. I approached and cleared my throat softly.

"I'm so sorry," I mumbled.

Not very reassuring, I know. But it was the truth. We—all of us— had let them down. It was our job to keep them safe, and we couldn't do it. It was our job not to let the mass slaughter of innocent children become our identity. It was our job to take action after the appalling tragedies at Sandy Hook Elementary and Columbine High, to protect their innocence, to shield them from this ugly reality. After Pulse, it was our job—*my job*—to ensure that no one else had to endure the hell that we had. Especially kids. But we fell short. I fell short.

"I'm sorry we failed you."

My head hung low, my stare piercing the toes of my dirty sneakers. I was ashamed to be seen like this, broken and incapable of inspiration. I couldn't bear to see the pain of their disappointment when they real- ized that the change we'd promised to bring about had been an utter failure. In some twisted way, I felt responsible for what had happened to them. If I'd just worked a little harder, their friends might still be here, and they might be worried about studying for the SATs, not trying to rewrite the law. I shuffled my feet nervously and lifted my gaze to meet theirs. What I saw caught me by surprise. There was no disappointment on their faces. No anger or frustration. They weren't scowling in judgment or frowning with skepticism. Every young face was steeled with resolve. They weren't afraid or defeated. They were determined. Ironically, they seemed intent on comforting *me*.

The circle parted just a bit, and a pair of arms pulled me into its center. Surrounded by a group of young students I had only just met, wrapped in their collective hug, words escaped me. I had been urged to give them some rousing, inspirational speech. I had armored myself, afraid to let them see me crying and in pain. And now they were shielding and consoling me, assuring me that my job wasn't to hoist the weight of the world onto my own shoulders and carry it on their behalf. My job was to trust them with my vulnerability. To show them that they weren't alone. To commit to being an accomplice in their work. And whatever the setbacks along the way, to never be dissuaded from making good on my promise to Drew.

We stood there for several minutes, though it may as well have been hours, before a young girl finally lifted her head and looked at me intently. "You can't give up," she said defiantly. "Because we're going to win."

Three years after the shooting, I was the first one from our community invited to testify before a congressional committee. I tried to play it cool before we slid into our seats, but it took everything in my power to keep the tremors in my hands from overcoming me. I sipped from a paper cup brimming with scorching coffee, shallow gulps scalding the top of my tongue, and chattered incessantly to keep my mind from racing. An aide cracked open the door and motioned us inside. I shuffled in, relieved to sit down and hide my quivering legs under a desk.

"No drinks inside," the aide snapped. I glanced down at my reflection in the deep brown ripples of my coffee before reluctantly tossing it in a trash can. *I'll have to find something else to fidget with,* I thought.

The hall was cavernous and lavishly appointed. Deep-blue curtains hung along the towering walls, a garnish of gold scalloped across the top. Matching navy-blue carpet was woven with an ornate pattern. The short wooden partitions that separated members of Congress from their constituents and journalists furiously clacking on their laptop keyboards were freshly polished and gleaming in the overhead stage lights. The grandeur of it all—bright lights, vibrant colors, the prestige of those in attendance—did nothing to help my buzzing nerves. I poured a glass of water from a pitcher on the desk and took a sip.

My prepared remarks flowed easily. I carefully recounted my standard routine of going out for a drink with Drew and Juan, the ordinary way in which our last night together had initially unfolded. I choked back tears as I relived the instant that gunfire first rang out, and the call to Juan's family to tell them their son had been shot. I begged them to hear our pleas and act, to stop making excuses and, as our leaders, do something to keep us safe. There were respectful nods. A reverent silence. Even the Republican members of the committee quietly absorbed the gut-wrenching stories laid before them, never glancing at their watches or scanning their phones. It felt like progress.

Then Congressman Kelly spoke. The ranking member of the committee was a stoic man in a loose-fitting suit. His lips pursed as he launched into a scathing response to our testimonies. With his glasses perched lightly near the end of his nose, he scoffed at our demands for Congress to act and all but cackled at the idea of focusing on legislative reforms. His voice dripped with disdain, even as his expression remained deadpan.

"Why wait around for others to do something?" he pressed. "Rather than expecting someone else to solve things, why not go improve your communities yourselves?"

My nervousness was immediately replaced by a wave of anger and astonishment. Part of me had assumed that politicians save their most callous performances for cable news. Desperate to see their names trend on Twitter or to inspire a witty chyron, they transform into diabolical caricatures only for prime time. But I couldn't have been more wrong. Every bit of the congressman's job was an act. While I had bared my soul, his quiet nods were a mere formality, hurrying me toward my conclusion. My story had not moved him. He had come to the hearing with his mind already made up, ready to regurgitate tired talking points so that his staff could pull C-SPAN clips for social media before happy hour. I was furious.

My heart thumped in my ears. I stared angrily at the furrowed brow behind the dais. "I hear you when you say that we have a responsibility to grow a culture of inclusion in our communities," I shot back, emotions brimming just beneath the surface. "That's what we've been doing. It's why I left a career in business to work for a nonprofit—so I can do exactly what you're talking about." The congressman's face remained unchanged, his mouth frozen into a scowl. "But that doesn't absolve this body, or the folks who are in elected office, from their responsibility."

In another life, I would have been embarrassed by my outburst. I would have spent the remainder of the day replaying every word in my head, pummeling my self-esteem to ash. But I felt emboldened, unafraid of the unvarnished honesty in my words or the bite in my tone. I was unashamed of my directness and the flames of anger fueling me. This powerful man, dripping with privilege and reveling in the trappings of his position, needed someone to put reality in front of him. He deserved to be challenged, to be confronted by those he was dismissing. I was filled with relief and a sense of accomplishment. I had spoken truth, and not just on my own behalf. I had spoken truth in honor of Drew and Juan.

I felt powerful.

Purpose is a fickle friend. Just as soon as it lifts you up or lights a fire in your belly, it can drag you into burnout, torturing you with a perpetual sense of inadequacy and pushing you past your limits. I've watched more than a few people—people I deeply care for—swallowed whole by their desperate desire to save the world. It's just one more event, one more video call, one more project until they collapse under the weight of their own altruistic mission. Those of us with a deep sense of purpose set our sights on the highest peaks and often fall prey to a feeling of failure if we only get halfway up before having to call for reinforcements.

But purpose is also a powerful antidote to grief, a potent salve on the rawest of wounds. Finding purpose allowed me to crawl out from underneath a comforter and reenter society. When I whispered a quiet promise to Drew at his funeral service, I had assumed that it would at least propel me through the eulogy and maybe help me find the words to tell his story, regardless of who would listen. But discovering that purpose, and committing to a lifelong fight for something bigger than myself, gave me the audacity to sit before Congressman John Lewis's subcommittee and refuse to be patronized by the ranking Republican. It gave me the courage to tour the country for Senator Elizabeth Warren's presidential campaign, visiting college campuses to urge students to get involved. It gave me the iron stomach to stand alongside Drew's mother at the Democratic National Convention and look out on tens of thousands of people without vomiting. It gave me the wisdom to sit quietly when young advocates are discovering their power, so as not to miss an important lesson that they may teach me. It gave me the relationships necessary to launch The Dru Project, an organization that has kept the best parts of Drew alive. It gave me the patience to accept temporary defeats as a natural part of the journey toward bigger victories yet on the horizon.

Early on, my nightmares were like a kaleidoscope from hell, twisting me back to the darkest periods of my life. I relived New Year's Eve in Ben's apartment over and over again, paralyzed in the purgatory between sleep and waking, his hands on my shoulders, pushing me down into the soft mattress topper until it nearly suffocated me. I flashed back to

Mom's hospital room, the machines whirring furiously as they fought to keep her alive. I tried to call to her, though no sound came out, and reached for her hand as she dissolved into the stiff sheets, my feet frozen to the cold tiles beneath me. I lived the dark terror of Pulse, again and again, the rancid smell of blood choking my airways before I woke in a cold sweat, gasping for air. And perhaps more terrifying than any of those nightmares was the very real thought that maybe never waking up would be a preferable option.

But my newfound sense of purpose felt like a refuge. As it grew, the intensity of those nightmares, and the thoughts that lurked inside them, seemed to fade. It was as if, just as the dark void of grief threatened to swallow me whole, a lifeline appeared, a reason to believe that living was worth the struggle. That life—not just mine but our collective existence—was worth fighting for.

PART 3: OVERCOMING

CHAPTER 8

FORGIVENESS

I finished pulling on my new pastel-pink suit and straightened my tie in the hotel mirror. I'm not usually one to venture beyond neutral colors, favoring a crisp black or navy jacket over more colorful options. But this was a big gay fundraiser in Los Angeles, complete with a red carpet and A-list celebrities, and I wanted to avoid sticking out like a sore thumb. As I laced up my patent leather shoes, my mind wandered to Drew. I tried imagining how he would have responded to an invitation like this if the tables had been turned. Maybe he would have beamed excitedly, flinging blazers from his messy open-air closet until he found just the right one. Maybe he would already be scanning the party for cute boys, revving up his charm before sitting down to the appetizer. Or maybe he would have sighed in exasperation, content to stay home and host a *Mario Kart* tournament instead of polishing an old pair of loafers and wading through a sea of insufferable rich people. If he did decide to show up, there was no doubt he would have been beelining for the bar already, bouncing excitedly on the balls of his feet as he waited in line. I sighed, daydreaming wistfully about what might have been, and tied a double knot in my laces.

A few of us were being honored by a big media organization for working to ensure that the Pulse shooting was never forgotten and that the legacies of the victims lived on. I was working in Starbucks management at the time, a career I chose in the years after my knees and shins grew weary of dancing on concrete for Disney. And though corporate employment offered stability and financial freedom, I wanted to be doing more. So I began moonlighting as an activist, traveling around the country, sharing my story, and organizing in my own community. I got creative with paid days off, hopping red-eye flights after long days at work to bank as much time as possible for my newfound passion. I wrote speeches while balancing my laptop and paper cups full of stale coffee on a tiny seat-back tray. I joined volunteer boards and spent weekends bouncing from one community event to another. It didn't pay in dollars, but this new work was rewarding. I loved seeing others become obsessed with how they could effect change too. I got excited for every opportunity to immerse myself in other communities trying desperately to heal after tragedy. I longed for bigger stages with more chairs full of people eager to make the world better. Every bit of it fed my desire to feel purposeful. And in another context, I might have beamed with pride at the thought of being honored by a big, prestigious organization for what amounted to a time-consuming passion project. But the whole affair felt a little odd. A swanky party with celebrities was light-years removed from the hastily assembled community meetings, cheap folding chairs, and grocery-store cookies that had marked the path toward this night. I tugged on my tie. *Can't wait to get home.*

The elevators were big and crowded, invoking the nervous twitch in my hand. I was lucky to have avoided most physical signs of trauma after the shooting. Some weren't as fortunate, having been permanently disabled, forced to relearn motor functions and adapt to new ways of life. Countless others were left with debilitating mental repercussions that made daily life an excruciating nightmare. I seemed to have made it out mostly unscathed. But occasionally, something unexpected would surface. An unintentional flinch when a folding chair fell over. The subconscious need to map out every exit in a bustling bar. Torturous insomnia that made sleeping more than three hours at a time virtually impossible. And there was the twitch. Usually triggered by loud, chaotic crowds in tightly packed spaces, my hand would instinctively clench into a ball, my nails digging into my palm. Trying to calm it was futile. As if possessed by its own panicked need to escape, my fist would squeeze repeatedly, painful indents appearing on the soft flesh of my palm, until I could slip from the crowd and take a long, deep gulp of air. Pressed against the back wall of the elevator, I felt my hand begin to seize furiously. The doors slid open, and I nudged past the sequined gowns and satin suits toward the hotel.

"Orlando!" a voice shouted from across the red carpet. "You're up!"

A flustered staffer jostled us down the plush crimson rug toward a deep-blue backdrop with a jumble of corporate logos on it. Cameras whirred relentlessly, the flashes blinding me as we made our way slowly from one end of the carpet to the other. Photographers screamed things I couldn't make out over the thump of my heartbeat in my ears. It was totally disorienting. One survivor leaned heavily onto his cane, the weight of the crowd seeming to hang on the leg that had been shattered months earlier by a spray of bullets. Others glanced around nervously, unsure of which shrieking paparazzo to acknowledge first. I tried desperately not to grimace, forcing my lips into a grin and gritting my teeth. All the while, the anxious staffer continued to nudge us along. Photos were snapped, microphones shoved in our faces. One reporter began telling us that he had gone to school in Orlando, but before I could catch his name, we were whisked through a door and onto a sunny deck for the reception. A sharply dressed server had barely lifted a glass of champagne in my direction before I snatched it off the platter and took two long gulps.

I wished I felt as carefree as the people milling around me looked. I wished I didn't have to duck into a bathroom stall to tamp down my anxiety or tune out the flashbacks of raging gunfire while faking a smile. But I also couldn't imagine having to live like this every day, perpetually shadowed by a gaggle of nosy people, unable to shield myself from the uncomfortable curiosity of the world. I took another swig from my glass and unclenched my fist.

The performances wound to a close, and partygoers moved upstairs to a ballroom that had been transformed into a nightclub. The beat of the music thundered under our feet, radiating as we slowly climbed an escalator. At the top, a maze of banners and confetti emptied into a cavernous space with a DJ tucked on one side of a stage. I was nervous to cram in alongside all these people, daring my trauma to stay hidden as we bumped our way through the crowd under whirling disco balls and past gyrating strobe lights. But I wasn't going to get another night like this. *Drew would do it,* I thought. *So can you.*

I stepped over to a bar along a wall, just off the dance floor. I figured a drink in my hand could serve as a welcome distraction and provide an excuse to slip out the door if needed. The bartender must have noticed the strained enjoyment on my face because he glanced at me, nodded knowingly, and added an extra ounce of vodka to my cup. The drinks were taking the edge off, and I was grateful to find this unlikely ally armed with a bottle of Tito's. I slipped a dollar into the polished can on the ledge of the bar, silently thanking him for discreetly sensing my buzzing anxiety, and turned around. Another survivor had sidled up with a cane. He was braver than I was. The vibrant floral pattern on his suit had been the talk of the gala, with celebrities fawning over its brilliant pinks and deep purples. He didn't seem to struggle as much with the small talk. His smile glowed naturally, its warm gleam disarming and welcoming. His laugh was infectious, a deep bellow invoking a cascade of giggles from everyone around us. I envied how calm he seemed and wondered if he had somehow learned how to hide his anxiety better than I had. We chatted aimlessly, cackling about how different this world was from the one we had left hours before. At an event back home, our suits would have stolen the show. Here, we were small fish in a very deep pond. Unspoken was a mutual acknowledgment of how strange it was for Orlando to be honored in a space this foreign, even as our community struggled to find its footing and fight for the resources it deserved.

A few minutes later, a woman approached us, a full glass of wine sloshing in her hand. She was dressed as elegantly as the rest, her deep-sapphire dress contrasting with the pearl jewelry around her neck and wrists. She had clearly been enjoying the open bar: her lipstick was slightly smudged, and her eyes were glassy. Free of the heels she clutched in her hand, her bare feet massaged the carpet beneath them. She wobbled a little, prompting her sharply dressed partner to grab her elbow and steady her. I didn't recognize her, but by then, faces were beginning to run together. She took a long sip, stared me down, and parted her wine-stained lips to speak.

"You don't realize how lucky you are," she slurred, stumbling and regaining her balance.

I stared back, blinking rapidly. What the hell did that mean? I had spent most of the previous months learning how to anticipate and react to the unsolicited things people commonly blurted at me:

I was almost at Pulse that night too.

I didn't go through what you did, but let me tell you about something similar.

Were you shot?

Do you miss them?

It could have been me.

From nearly the beginning, I mastered the art of allowing others to offload their own traumas in an effort to find the right words. People seem to gravitate toward finding a shared emotion as a way of expressing sympathy. Admittedly, it's hard to know how to best respond when someone is working hard to sympathize with your pain as a show of support. But you *weren't* there. It *wasn't* you. And yes, I miss them.

Most people's experiences *aren't* all that similar. But they don't need to be for us to stand in solidarity. Nevertheless, I had learned to swallow biting retorts, appreciate the poorly communicated intent, and share sympathy in return. Normally, that was effective. But no one had ever called me "lucky" before. The woman must have noticed my quizzical expression.

"You don't realize how lucky you are to be standing next to such strength." Her words tumbled out of her mouth. She gestured to the boy next to me, her gaze slowly tracing the long line of his cane.

I understood what she was suggesting. His strength was clear from the outside. He had overcome debilitating physical injuries and learned to walk again. His shattered bones had been repaired, and he had learned to stand tall again, when most didn't think he ever would. He had beaten all the odds and made it through alive, pulled to safety by paramedics to undergo hours of intense surgery and terrifying blood loss. His survival was real, mine only anecdotal. From her vantage point, his strength was in his ability to push past the crushing pain and still find joy for life itself. His survival was strength. Mine was just good luck.

I clenched my jaw and nodded knowingly, hoping that she would move on. The boy next to me glanced at me nervously. He was clearly embarrassed, but neither of us had the energy to argue with her. *Better to let the bar continue to distract her,* I imagined us both thinking. The woman teetered forward, wrapping the other survivor in an awkward embrace and nearly knocking his cane out from under him. I could smell the alcohol on her breath as she muttered something in his ear. Then she wobbled off to the bar, leaving me stunned in her wake.

That experience shook me for quite some time. It even became the topic of my first op-ed, published by CNN in the summer of 2017. I wondered if she was right. Maybe I should be ceding the spotlight to those who were physically injured. After all, I left Pulse in a car that night, rather than being wheeled into the emergency room on a gurney.

Maybe she was right to question whether I was grateful enough to bear witness to the strength of those relearning to walk. Maybe all those nights spent alone in my apartment, wailing into my pillow, were little more than self-indulgence, a pattern of weakness. Maybe I would never know the strength of the boy leaning into his ornate cane and gliding from one camera to the next. Maybe I was being greedy by taking up my therapist's time when someone else needed it more. Maybe she was right. Maybe I didn't realize just how lucky I was.

Then again, maybe she wasn't. Who was a tipsy partygoer tottering around in a crushed velvet gown to decide what counts as valid survival—or strength? Why should I apologize for waking up every night in a cold sweat, crying out for those long gone? Why did I need a cane or gruesome X-rays to make the permanent damage real? Wasn't it enough that I couldn't be in a crowded bar without my fingernails digging into the palm of my hand, or that the sound of Drew's laughter had vanished from my apartment, from my life, leaving behind a hollow, silent hole?

As the days went on, I began to realize that these questions ran deeper. Paralyzing doubts chased me from sleep to waking and back again. I became acutely aware of the immense guilt I was lugging around like a brick tucked into my backpack. I felt guilty that I could still bound down the stairs in the morning, late for work, with a coffee in one hand and my phone jostling in the other, while others had to relearn how to put one foot in front of the other. I felt guilty that I could drown my feelings in the workday, furiously typing emails until long after the sun had gone down, while others couldn't. I felt guilty that although I wanted to be there for everyone around me, I was suffocating under the overwhelming weight of a world I no longer recognized. I felt guilty for making it out when others hadn't. For the families shattered by the loss of their babies, while my family had the luxury of carrying on as if nothing had happened. I felt guilty for being alive.

I pulled my stool closer to the kitchen island and nervously tugged my shirt into place. Multiple cameras and microphones were set up around me, boxing me into a tight square. I could see myself in the reflection of the camera lens in front of me, its curved lens exaggerating the love handles stretching the buttons of my shirt. I had gained a lot of weight, the result of using Sour Patch Kids and sparkling wine to numb the bits that my therapist hadn't uncovered yet. By this point, I had done countless interviews and knew how to recount my story without plunging so far into the most treacherous parts that I couldn't pull myself out. But for some reason, this one made me nervous. The straining buttons and round chin in the reflection weren't helping my confidence. I tugged at my shirt again.

The director was a gruff man, his mouth distorted into a permanent scowl that masked years of telling stories that had chipped away at his heart. He spent what seemed like hours fiddling with each camera, barking instructions at his crew, peering into a viewfinder, hunching back into his seat, and starting the process all over again. His chubby fingers scratched notes on a white pad on the counter, the letters barely legible. Just when I started to get restless, he would glance up and nod, encouraging me to continue.

Most interviews about the shooting are tedious exercises in reliving my experience, over and over again, so that a self-important journalist can repackage it with new cover art. They all take mostly the same tack. The directors swagger with confidence, launching into a litany of questions. "Can you take me back to that night?" they ask. "How do you feel when you revisit Pulse?"

I don't betray my annoyance at their lack of creativity and calmly recount the night that changed my life. Back and forth we go. Their eyebrows rise in surprise. They compliment my composure, how "articulate" I am. I nod graciously. Neither of us admits that these surface-level questions have been asked and answered dozens of times before. Newer interviewers fumble for the next questions when their prepared lists are exhausted. The more seasoned are equipped with a few thoughtful follow-ups. I perfected this dance early on, learning to retell the darkest parts of my nightmare without dissolving into a pathetic puddle of emotion.

This interview began in much the same way. Despite his rough exterior, the director was kind. Occasionally, he nodded with encouragement. He would peek down briefly, dragging his pencil across the page, then peer back up at me over the rim of his thick glasses. We started off with the usual questions. Then he asked about Drew. And about Juan. He wondered aloud what had brought me thousands of miles from home to Orlando. He wanted to know what was special about Pulse, why I kept calling it a safe space. I responded to each question, carefully weaving the tale of chosen family, grief, and renewed purpose that I knew like the back of my hand.

Midway through the interview, he paused to change a camera battery. The mood in the apartment was light and cheerful. On a short couch a few feet away, my friends listened intently, nodding as the director and I crafted the story together. One was curled up in a soft armchair, buried in her phone. The director flitted around, fiddling with knobs and peering into lenses. When he returned to his seat, his forehead scrunched a bit. He glanced up from his notes and sighed.

"I'm going to ask you something," he said softly. "And I don't want you to feel like you have to answer if it's too painful."

"I'm sure I can handle it," I blurted, chuckling nervously.

"I want to know if you feel guilty," he said bluntly. He shuffled in his seat, and a pregnant pause hung over us all. "I suppose what I'm asking is, do you feel responsible for what happened to your friends? Because you invited them out that night?"

For the first time in an interview, I was speechless. In an instant, I was transported back to the fancy afterparty in Los Angeles. The woman in the crushed velvet dress stood in front of me, wine still sloshing in her glass, telling me how lucky I was, asking me if I was even worth the gift of survival. She scorched a hole through me, her intense stare clawing for more. Who did I think I was, moving on, finding normalcy again? Didn't I feel shame?

The image of the woman burned away, leaving me back in the kitchen full of cameras. The silence was deafening. A camera operator shifted his weight. Another cleared his throat.

The question stunned me, not just because no one had ever asked it before but because I'd been too afraid to ask it myself. Yes, I *did* feel guilty. I felt that, in some way, I had stolen a life from one of the bodies now resting in a cemetery across town. I was ashamed of getting up in the morning, putting on a freshly ironed shirt, and going to work as if none of it had ever happened while Drew's and Juan's families fought to put the shattered pieces of their lives back together. And I felt guilty that were it not for one late-afternoon text to my best friends—were I not so caught up in trying to win over a boy—they would still be here. For the first time, I came face-to-face with the fear that I had killed Drew and Juan.

I looked up at the director. His menacing scowl had melted away, and his expression was pained. My mind raced with all the things I wanted to tell him. I thought of Drew's mother sitting just a few feet away. I wanted to scream at the top of my lungs that I had cost her child the rest of his life, that I was sorry. I wanted to stare into my own reflection and beg for forgiveness for not going back in to save them. I wanted to tell God right then and there that he should have taken me instead. I started to sob uncontrollably. I had so many things I wanted to say, so much I needed to confess, but I couldn't find the words to begin.

The crew clicked the cameras off, mercifully trying to give me space to compose myself. I took deep, slow breaths, trying to calm my shaking shoulders and regain control over my trembling jaw. Someone handed me a crumpled napkin to wipe my eyes, which smudged the concealer I had used to mask the dark circles under them. Eventually my tears subsided, and the bright lamps were switched back on. I squared my shoulders, apologizing for having subjected them to an utter meltdown, and indicated to the director that I was ready.

The words nearly tumbled out of my mouth. "I do feel guilty," I blurted. My hand clenched instinctively. "I feel like I killed them both. And I just wish their families knew how sorry I am for what I've done to them."

The most important revelations I've had over the years rarely come during a therapy session or from an overpriced self-help book served up in my feed by the Instagram algorithm. Don't get me wrong. Professional help—external help—has been an important component of my healing. But the most important self-discoveries have occurred at junctures like that one—unexpected collisions with vulnerability that force me to confront the darkest elements of my own mind. Asked with half a dozen cameras aimed in my direction, a single question unlocked new answers about what life after tragedy might look like. For the first time, I said out loud the words that had silently haunted me. I called my most petrifying demons into the light, named them, and reclaimed my power over them in front of a stunned group of friends. Once the words had escaped my mouth, I realized that my guilt was a self-imposed burden. That I had to choose not to carry it any longer. And that, whenever I was ready, I could begin the work of relieving myself of it.

I chose to forgive myself that day. For finding joy again in a world that is joyless for so many. For singing and laughing and dancing and loving when others will never get the chance to do that again. I chose to forgive myself for that night at Ben's apartment, for being too paralyzed by fear to fight back and too ashamed to scream for help. I chose to forgive myself for needing support in order to feel whole again, for feeling merely squeezed by the grip of my trauma while others were still being suffocated by theirs. I chose to forgive myself for surviving that night at Pulse. For moving forward. For stopping to smell the sweet flowers at the grocery store and basking in the warmth of the summer sun. For waking up every morning, even though the people I loved most won't ever wake again. In forgiveness, I gave myself permission to live again. To laugh again. To love again.

I'm not responsible for what happened to forty-nine people in a dark club on a summer night in 2016. I'm not responsible for the pain inflicted on their families, friends, and loved ones. I'm not responsible for the deaths of Drew and Juan. The sole person responsible for that horror is the man who pulled the trigger. My only job now is to carry on the best parts of my best friends, to live a life full of the hope and joy that was stolen from them as they stood wrapped in each other's arms. Finally, confronted with my deepest shame but refusing to be held hostage by it any longer, I let its grip on me loosen, just a bit.

~

A knot settled firmly in the pit of my stomach as I pulled my car into the lot at Dad's hotel. I had lived for more than a decade in Orlando, and he was visiting me for the first time. I'd painstakingly planned a few days of activities: Dad had once dreamed of being an astronaut, a vision ended by a health crisis in college, so I got tickets to the Kennedy Space Center. I drew up plans to visit theme parks, eat at some of my favorite restaurants, and introduce friends to the man they had heard so much about. I've always loved playing host and wanted him to find the same joy in my city as I had. But I was most eager to show off the full life that I had created for myself. I imagined that he still saw me as an obstinate teenager, slamming doors and playing music too loudly. So much had changed. I had a good job. A nice car. My own apartment. Stability. I wanted him to see me all grown up, to give him permission to be proud of the man I had become.

I was nervous too. It had been years since we spent meaningful time together, most of which were marked by tense, fractured communication. Would we have the language to speak to one another? I couldn't help but think back to the long car ride to college, the mile markers whizzing by the window. I was seething then, incapable of finding the words to tell him how I felt. Did he remember that drive? Did it still feel like yesterday for him too?

The glass doors of the hotel slid open, and he stepped out onto the concrete. My stepmom had warned me that he was growing a new beard, but it was much more impressive in real life. He was, in many ways, exactly like I remembered. He still strutted with intense purpose, his hands jammed into the front pockets of his jeans while his short legs churned underneath him. It had always seemed like he was in a hurry, even when we didn't have anywhere to be. He still tucked his *Star Wars* T-shirt neatly into a pair of faded blue jeans and fastened his worn leather belt tightly. He still giggled as he crossed in front of a stopped car, nervously thanking the driver for ceding the right of way. But he had also changed. His eyes were wearier, the weight of raising children and growing older having dimmed their shine just a bit. Wrinkles had formed on his forehead, and deep crow's feet now tugged at the skin near his temples. Years of working overtime in the harshest elements had weathered his once youthful skin. He was a union man working full time for the local power company, and the long hours rebuilding broken power poles had calloused the palms of his hands. His long hair, once blond and well kept, had given way to brilliant grays and whites. His energy was somehow both familiar and foreign, like a worn page from a beloved children's book, its story a distant dream. He opened the car door and slid onto the leather seat.

I began babbling incoherently the second he closed the door. I laid out our plan for the week, excitedly bouncing from one destination to the next. The Space Coast. Cinderella Castle. My favorite Malaysian restaurant. At every stop, I gleefully pointed out how it had been inspired by something he liked to do or offered a new adventure I wanted to expose him to. He alternated between listening intensely and chuckling graciously, clearly overwhelmed by my hyperactive rundown of our agenda. I paused to take a breath, realizing I had rambled for some time.

Dad cleared his throat. "It all sounds wonderful, son," he said quietly. He sounded genuinely grateful for my meticulous game plan, but a *but* was imminent. "But what I'm most excited about is spending a few days in your life."

I didn't immediately respond. It's true that everything I had put together was of some interest to me. I had never gone to see the shuttle *Atlantis*. My handpicked restaurants were places I liked to treat myself to on lazy weekends. And it had been years since I enjoyed an afternoon at a theme park, despite living just down the street from Disney. But nothing I rattled off to Dad reflected the unvarnished truth about who I had become. There were no gay bars on the docket, no packed brunch spots with drag queens whirling by the tables to snatch crumpled dollar bills from outstretched hands. There were no game nights with my friends, no drunken confessions from the cute bartender at our favorite Sunday haunt. Years later, I was still tucked behind the curtain, pulling levers, manipulating smoke and mirrors to avoid giving him an authentic taste of the man I had become. I was still shielding him from the parts of my life that I thought he might be embarrassed by.

"You're right. That would be nice."

By that time, nothing was more authentically me than squeezing in an interview before lunch, a chore I was sure Dad would find utterly uninteresting. We drove to the Four Seasons, an ornate hotel in a forested part of town near the theme parks. A man with a glimmering name tag rushed to open the car doors, his free arm outstretched toward the building, which was undoubtedly one of the nicest places I had ever been. The doorway was flanked by sandy stone pillars. Grand hallways jutted in opposite directions from the lobby. Soft classical music played from speakers as well-dressed staff bustled from one guest to the next. We had never stayed anywhere like this as kids. Dad was always mindful of money and obsessed with obscure adventures, preferring to cram the family into spare bedrooms at Grandma's house or to camp on some remote plot of land. This was a far cry from homemade pancake mix grilled over an open flame outside my little plastic tent.

We followed the winding hallway toward the balcony we'd been assigned for our interview. It was lined with towering arched windows draped in long, neutral-colored curtains. The view was tranquil. Trees swayed in a light breeze. Birds bounced from branch to branch. We stepped through a tall door and out onto a shaded, neatly outfitted terrace. Plush couches and soft-looking chairs circled the marble walkway. In the center sat one long sofa, surrounded by a few lighting rigs. A single camera pointed toward the oversize cushions.

Tyler and Raymond, storytellers best known for mastering witty. YouTube content at the platform's inception, jumped up from one end of the couch and rushed over to welcome us with hugs and handshakes. They were a funny pair. Tyler was short and bubbly, while Raymond stood taller and was more understated. Both brimmed with excitement, which helped to ease my anxiety just a bit. And they were both unapologetically gay, whispering and giggling about the latest pop culture headlines. We had never met before, but it felt like I had known them for a lifetime.

They introduced themselves to Dad, gesturing to the seats spread haphazardly around the balcony and warmly inviting him to pick the one that seemed most comfortable. I had only briefly explained the plan, and I slightly regretted thrusting him into this situation. We hadn't spent much time getting to know each other again, and I wasn't sure how he felt about diving headfirst into this part of my life. But I knew one thing for certain: spending an afternoon at a fancy resort hotel with three gay boys was sure to leave him feeling like a fish out of water. He picked a seat a few feet from where the camera sat, a perfect angle to watch our conversation, and slumped back against the armrest. The boys prepped and preened, fastening a microphone to my collar and tugging on their clothes to flatten any wrinkles. With the camera in place and all of us settled, the interview began.

The conversation flew by, minutes melting into hours until we reached the breathless end. We breezed through milestones, making pit stops at important parts of the story line and U-turns to linger at the places that always choked me up. It was like I was chatting with a couple of old friends over a glass of wine. I felt safe telling Tyler and Raymond the hardest parts of what had brought us together. My story somehow felt like it belonged to them too. I confessed how hard it had been to lose my mom and feel like a stranger in my childhood home. We giggled like schoolgirls when I admitted that, before we became best friends, I was convinced an Instagram boy named Drew was my soul mate. We beamed as we talked about our chosen families, who were like a queer secret weapon we were proud to show off. By the time we got to Drew's polished casket, halfway down the aisle of a stunning cathedral in downtown Orlando, all three of us were in tears.

I had become so engrossed in bringing my new friends on this journey that I had forgotten my dad sitting a few feet away. I peeked over the camera and saw him staring down at his feet. He seemed enraptured by the fraying toes of his sneakers, and his signature expression was unchanged from when we had stepped out of the car. I had no idea how any of this was landing with him—whether he was upset with me for airing shreds of our dirty laundry or felt an ounce of sympathy for what I'd been through, his heart aching somewhere behind a mask of chiseled stone.

Tyler switched the camera off, his goofy smirk reappearing, and pushed his oversize glasses up past his eyebrows. He thanked me and pulled me in for a tight hug, his squeeze like a silent affirmation of our newfound bond. Raymond did the same, and our lighthearted conversation trailed off. They drifted over to Dad and stood sheepishly in front of him.

"I'm sorry if that was a lot," Tyler said awkwardly.

Dad chuckled nervously and nodded. "I actually wanted to thank you," he said. "I think we needed that."

Things were quiet when we got back into the car. I hoped that my phone would ring, giving me an excuse to do anything but rehash what had just happened. I hadn't intended for him to be force-fed my ugly memories of our relationship, but a part of me was glad he'd sat through it. For the first time, he was forced to live through me. No carefully constructed image. No opportunity for defiant interjection. He had been forced to sit in silence and see me—the whole me. I don't know that I ever would have found the courage to tell him all those things so honestly. I don't know that I ever would have shared with him how hard it was for me growing up. He would have never known how close I came to ending my own life before packing two suitcases and taking a leap of faith. I would have been content to keep those bits from him, to avoid them forever. But now that the words still hung uncomfortably between us, I was glad he had finally heard them.

Dad cleared his throat and shuffled his feet. "Son," he said abruptly, his customary way of indicating that what came next was important, "I want you to take me to Pulse."

I can't remember how I reacted. To this day, the whole idea of it still catches me by surprise. This was the same man who had been utterly disgusted with me after learning that I liked boys. The same man who could hardly contain his contempt on the phone. The man whose temper terrified me, and whose approval seemed impossible to earn. I had wanted him to *see me* for so long that I didn't consider what it would feel like if it actually happened. So I obliged, and I pulled onto the highway.

The early-summer sun was beating down by the time we arrived at Pulse. Beads of sweat had formed above Dad's unkempt brows. Ripples of heat radiated up from the asphalt. In a nearby tree, a few cicadas buzzed loudly, their tune unchanged by the hallowed ground beneath them. The site was empty and still, the dark towering walls of the club tucked behind a chain-link fence encased in black fabric. Along the fence, people from across the world had placed flowers and gifts in honor of the lives that had been stolen inside. Plastic pinwheels and rainbow flags, once crisp and vibrant, had faded under the harsh glare of the Florida sun. We walked slowly past the bits of memorabilia: photos left behind by loved ones, birthday cards, Christmas gifts. The joyful smiles of the victims frozen, as if no time had passed at all. Dad was stoic. He always kept his emotions tightly bottled, loath to show cracks in his tough, battered armor. Through the dark tint of his sunglasses, I could see him squinting to take it all in. He paused at a poster with the names and pictures of the forty-nine victims, scanning each one carefully.

The infamous sign near the edge of the property had been transformed into a community message board with notes and words of love.

Dad picked up a fine-point marker and scribbled a few words on the worn paint. I couldn't make out what it said, but it didn't matter. That he thought to write anything was enough. We walked slowly from one end of the lot to the other, pausing occasionally as I explained how it had been before the tragedy. I took him to the back of the building, where we peeked through a hole in the fence at the place where police had used explosives to breach the walls and free hostages huddled around leaky toilets. I showed him the route I had taken, the spot where I knelt on the sidewalk and called him just before 3:00 a.m. I pointed through a split in the fabric at the exit through which I had escaped that night, its doors still riddled with bullet holes. All the while, his demeanor remained unchanged. His lips were pursed, his brow deeply furrowed.

As we made our way back toward the car, he stopped at a photo of Drew and Juan that hung from the fence by two zip ties. He lingered on their blissful grins, their innocent happiness still palpable despite the weathered paper. I could see that, for the first time, he was processing what it must have been like for them. For me. I wondered what he thought about all of it. Was he trying to imagine the horrors of that night? To comprehend what their deaths sounded and smelled like? Was he trying to picture what it must have been like for me, crouched against the wall, listening to a hail of gunfire outside? Could he hear the wails of other parents howling like wounded dogs? Was he sad? Mad? Or just struggling with the overwhelming inability to articulate a potent cocktail of emotions?

We slid into the car and clicked the doors closed behind us. The rush of cold air from the vents provided relief and some sound to interrupt the silence. I glanced over to see a single tear falling down Dad's cheek. I've always considered his hardened exterior to be a strength. He's not overcome by things like I am. He always found a way to grit his teeth and pull through anything, holding the family together by shoestrings when it seemed inevitable that we'd come apart at the seams. He used to scoff when I would burst into tears as a kid, barking at me to "cut the waterworks" and storming out with a huff. But here in the car, he was refreshingly human. At his request, we'd come to my most vulnerable place, and he didn't revert to the man I had once resented and often feared. He allowed himself to be vulnerable alongside me, exposing his pain as if it were an offering of peace and reconciliation. I instinctively looked down at my hands, a reflexive attempt to avoid getting caught staring. I wanted him to know how much I appreciated him while still allowing him the space to feel it all. I started the ignition, determined to let the silence persist if he needed it. But before we could pull away, he cleared his throat.

"Son," he said, his voice wavering, "I am so sorry you had to go through this. That your friends had to go through this. I know I said and did things when you were a kid that were hurtful. Truthfully, I was scared. Scared that the world wouldn't understand you. Scared that the world would hurt you. I realize now that I wasn't ever going to stop bad things from happening. I just ensured that when those bad things happened, you didn't feel like you could call me first."

My understanding of forgiveness has evolved over time. Sitting at a countertop across from a film director, I learned that forgiveness is not just an olive branch we extend to others but a necessary first step to healing ourselves. And sitting with my father, the man I harbored the most resentment toward, I understood forgiveness to be not a dismissal of past harm but an offer of grace and a chance to create something new. I used to hold on to toxic grudges because I wanted people to pay for what they had done, and forgiving them felt like injustice. But in truth, offering them grace allowed me to lift from my shoulders the burden of what *had been* in order to leave space for what *could be*.

In a moment of intense vulnerability, as a cold blast of air-conditioning dried the tears on our cheeks, I forgave my dad. He didn't ask or expect me to. I can't remember if I'd ever said those words—*I forgive you*—to him before. But I made a choice that day to refuse to carry the weight of our rocky relationship anymore. Every one of us is human. We make mistakes. We fail. We learn. We grow. We hurt people. Sometimes we go back to make things right, and those times have to mean something. When I talked back to my mother, defiantly wagging my finger at her, she forgave me. When I lashed out at Drew in a fit of jealousy, my drunken envy bubbling over in a crowded nightclub, he forgave me too. Because forgiveness is not just an offer of grace—it is a powerful act of unconditional love.

Forgiveness is hard and messy. Sometimes it's two steps forward. Other times, three steps back. But it offers a deeply powerful beginning that can chart a whole new path forward.

I don't know how many more birthday cards I'll get from Dad before he's gone. I don't know how many more monogrammed Christmas gifts will come in the mail. But I know that life is terrifyingly short. And though Dad wasn't entitled to it, forgiving him was a necessary step toward realizing the full power of my own potential.

He hurt me over the years. Sometimes it was in little ways: unnecessary disappointment over a single B on my report card, irritated combativeness when I couldn't keep up during a political debate. Other times he cut more deeply. The way he rejected me when I was at my most vulnerable as a queer teenager spiraling out of control. His sharp tongue when I dared to challenge him, the words he chose slicing like a knife. His inability to see how isolating it was for me to wander the world alone, a half-Black kid called "Oreo cookie" and "little monkey" at school, without anyone to tell me how to condition my curly hair or moisturize my ashy elbows. His thick emotional shell—a survival mechanism constructed to protect himself after Mom died—that kept him from hugging me as often as I needed. We talked past each other for years, and I held a grudge for even longer. But it was time to let go. We were grown men, with more than a lifetime of lessons learned between us, finally willing to let down our guards in a quiet bit of honesty. We weren't sparring minds anymore.

We were simply father and son, an imperfect family, content to be just that—a family.

I let out a sigh and choked back a decade's worth of tears.

Dad turned to me, now beaming with pride. "I love you, son."

And I believed him.

CHAPTER 9

CARPE DIEM

Giving yourself permission to live again can open myriad doors, which take on different shapes and meanings depending on the circumstances. Sometimes it's as simple as finding the courage to go sit at your favorite corner table again and savor a glass of wine. Other times it's more significant, like allowing yourself to kiss, date, and fall in love again after the loss of a partner. I dared myself to go on an adventure, the kind that Drew and Juan loved to plan with almost no notice. Eric and I finally broke up in the fall of 2017, and I took it as a sign. He was, in many ways, the last tie that bound me to the heavy burden I felt—the responsibility to carry the weight of the shooting with me. It seemed as if the universe, or whatever greater power, was done gently nudging me back out into the world and had decided to give me one last shove.

I had lost myself in the rat race, pouring every ounce of my being into the work of creating a legacy for others. Up to that point, forgiving myself felt much more like penance. I was trapped on a hamster wheel, churning my legs furiously only to end up right back where I started. It felt as though I could only be granted my own forgiveness when I became *worthy* of it, as if I had to save the world to earn back my place in it. There was incredible personal reward in that work, but there wasn't always joy in it. I missed exploring unknown corners, diving face-first into a plate of food I didn't recognize, wandering streets with names I couldn't pronounce in a place where I didn't know the language. I missed the pure, unadulterated joy of being alive. No responsibilities. No to-do lists. No impostor syndrome clouding my head, no dread that I'll be discovered. Just the smell of velvety summer air, soft grass under my toes. I wanted to get past the idea of earning my own forgiveness and learn to live unapologetically again. So I began jotting down corners of the world I had always dreamed of visiting.

For some people, the prospect of turning thirty is almost debilitating. The hangovers linger, and the pounds don't fall off like they used to. Turning the page on a decade can be an understandably scary milestone for anyone, and even more so for gay men. The community is hopelessly obsessed with holding on to its youth, petrified of the wrinkles and sagging skin that come with age. At thirty years old, a gay man might as well cosplay as Gandalf the White, roaring in on his trusty steed for the final battle in *The Lord of the Rings*, his frosty, unkempt beard flailing in the wind. So it's unsurprising that I was petrified of crossing that threshold, worried about whether I would become obsolete, traded in for a newer, fresher model. But I was excited too. About starting a new chapter. About turning a metaphorical page. It seemed like the right time to rediscover myself, to give myself permission for new adventures and new connections.

I sat in the noisy corner of a Starbucks store in rural Tallahassee. The bustle provided a welcome distraction from the stress of a long week at work. I clicked aimlessly on my computer, scanning monotonous piles of spreadsheets and graphs, my productivity sapped. There is immense stability in a nine-to-five corporate job, but it tends to drag at the end of the week. I casually browsed flights out of Orlando. My birthday was around the corner, and I'd been talking about scratching one of the cities off my dream list. They varied in distance and difficulty, from English-speaking burgs near home to distant cities with unfamiliar skylines and street signs in new languages. It almost didn't matter where—I was just ready to write a fresh page in a place unlike home.

I refreshed the page and, to my surprise, discovered that tickets to France were just a few hundred dollars. I had frantically tracked my checking-account balance and bought gas with coins from beneath seat cushions for so long that it hadn't crossed my mind that international travel would ever be within my price range. My finger hovered nervously over the "Enter" key. It had been a long time since I'd done something impulsive, let alone something that served no other purpose than to treat myself. But growing, moving on, occasionally requires a leap of faith. I pressed the key and held my breath. One flight to Paris. Happy birthday to me.

I rented a tiny apartment in the heart of the city, its balcony hanging above a busy street lined with brightly colored shop windows. It was on the fourth floor of an old building without a working elevator. It was cozy and modestly outfitted, with a well-appointed kitchen separated from the dimly lit living room by an oversize, American-style island. A low, modern couch sat facing a pair of tall glass doors that opened onto a cramped balcony above the courtyard. Settling in was my first order of business. I unpacked bags and stuffed drawers, neatly organizing twice as many outfits as I needed. The summer weather was mild, cool enough to fling open the windows and fall asleep with a gentle breeze drifting through the long, sheer curtains. In the morning, the smell of freshly baked bread wafted through the open doors from the boulangerie downstairs, rousing me just after sunrise and nudging me toward the coffee maker.

The nearby grocery store stocked warm baguettes, steam still rising from their golden crusts, and displayed fresh fruit in the window. I picked out a few plump oranges and the thickest loaf of bread, then scraped together a handful of coins and placed them on the counter, sheepishly wishing the cashier a good morning in broken French. A few doors down, a chocolate shop had bottles of perfectly dry, crisp wine on the shelves. I stuffed a few into my reusable shopping bag, then huffed and heaved up the narrow staircase in my apartment building, shopping bags draped over each arm. I got lost on more than one occasion, wandering down cobblestone side streets and past centuries-old churches. I sipped espresso at a corner coffee shop, watching carefree Parisians as they strolled the sidewalks with thin cigarettes dangling from their lips. There was peace in being nameless and storyless, thousands of miles from home.

I experienced deep joy and healing in Paris. I stopped to smell a patch of flowers. I sat on a park bench, my phone left behind in the apartment, and watched families play with paper boats in a gurgling fountain, content to enjoy their cheerful obliviousness from afar. I walked without a destination and ate food without first scanning the menu online. No thesis project, no voter files. I sang, danced, and laughed without once thinking about all the work I could be burying myself in.

One afternoon, I sauntered aimlessly down a quiet side street, the crumbling walls of an old building brushing my left arm. The sun was high in a clear blue sky, and a gentle breeze ambled. A few paces in front of me, an old woman meandered casually. She was short but not frail, her sturdy frame rooted in broad, strong shoulders. She wore a vibrant floral-print dress that swayed at the ankles as she walked and a thin, brightly colored scarf in her hair. After a few paces, a scrap of plastic fluttering on the sidewalk caught her attention. She slowed, bent down, and picked it up. She glanced around, spotted a trash can a few feet away and walked back to it, gently tossing the wrapper into the can, then practically glowing with pride. I imagined that she had lived on this block her whole life, that generations of her family had called it home. I imagined that this was part of her routine: a late afternoon stroll to her favorite pastry shop, occasional interruptions to keep the neighborhood clean. I imagined that her family had owned a local restaurant and taught her to tidy tables and greet customers at a young age. I imagined how proud she must be to call such a beautiful place home.

She looked up at me with a glint in her eye. "Bonjour!" she exclaimed sweetly.

"Good morn—er, bonjour!" I replied in a garbled American accent.

She giggled politely, spun on her heels, and continued ahead. A smile formed on my lips, and its warmth spread down my neck and through my body. Before I knew it, I had erupted into laughter. Not a judgmental cackle or nervous chuckle but a full-throated, intensely jubilant giggle. My shoulders shook, and my sides ached as I doubled over. The encounter had filled me with unanticipated joy.

It wasn't the first time I'd laughed since Pulse, but it was the first laugh I remember vividly. There was such an intensity to its release, like my spirit had peeked out for an instant to assess whether it was finally safe to come out. Up to that point, joy had invoked a deep sense of guilt. After all, Drew and Juan would never get to experience it again. They would never laugh. Or feel. They would never dance. Or sing. Their lights had been snuffed out, their last sounds a chorus of screams for mercy. As a result, it felt like I was condemned to an eternity of hollow sadness and a joyless obsession with work, just to *earn* more time on earth. I loaded weekends with events and meetings. I felt shame in taking a day off. I maintained a never-ending Facebook stream of all the things I was accomplishing, avoided posting anything that made me appear to be enjoying life, and worried that trolls would descend and question why I wasn't trapped in a perpetual purgatory of mourning. I watched them do it to others, torturing school-shooting survivors for sharing a day at the beach or a collection of photos from graduation. But I wasn't just running from the relentless Twitter mob; I was punishing myself. I tried desperately not to feel joy because it didn't seem right when every new day that I woke to felt stolen.

But that laugh—that brief, unguarded, vulnerable happiness—felt different. I was happy, and the world had continued to spin. Far from home, where I'd been subject to prying gazes and saturated in escapable reminders of all that had happened, I lifted the veil, just a little. I dared myself to live.

I met a boy in Paris too. Michael. I have no idea how I'd go about finding him again. But I remember how his tousled curls bounced when

I first noticed him. How he smelled when I pressed him close on a dance floor. How free I felt in his arms. By chance, I had bumped into a few American friends at a bar just a couple of blocks from my downtown apartment. It was a sketchy underground joint, with a narrow, rickety stairwell descending into the dark, hazy halls of the club below. I nearly bolted for an exit, but then I saw a familiar face and slid onto a stool behind the bar. My friends were in town from New York City for a few days and invited me to join them at a party later that night.

Traveling solo, halfway across the globe, already tested the bounds of my social skills. I spent my first night in Paris eating pulverized pretzels from my luggage because I feared that if I attempted to order food at a restaurant, I would mangle the words on the menu and be laughed out the door. So my initial instinct when invited to a random party in some distant corner of town was to decline politely, then wander the bustling streets on my own, with no obligation to do anything that might force me to talk to anyone else. How do you strike up a conversation at a party in a foreign country? How long before a stranger grimaces and walks away while you fumble with Google Translate? *Not worth it,* I thought. But I paused, took a sip from my glass, and scolded myself for losing sight of the purpose of my trip. This was about ridding myself of self-imposed bonds, about diving into the deep end and finding a way to swim.

Stop making excuses and grow a pair.

I agreed to meet my friends at the location, then scribbled the address onto a nearby cocktail napkin and shoved it into my pocket.

Always ask more questions than you think are necessary. That's the first lesson of this story. I had imagined a modest house party with a dozen or so people milling about a private, expensive row house in the posh suburbs. The party was actually a rave in a cavernous warehouse on a run-down block in the heart of the city. My concerns about being able to banter in a foreign language were misplaced. It wouldn't have been possible to talk above the din, but that concern was replaced by overwhelming anxiety about losing my friends in the abyss, coupled with a healthy dose of crippling body dysmorphia. The building was a labyrinth of washboard abs and short shorts. In the back was a row of bars where I spent most of my night, leveraging them as both an excuse to avoid wading through the crowd of sweaty bodies and a perfect vantage point from which to identify all the exits. A large stage on the opposite wall was the only landmark in an otherwise expansive box. I tried easing my anxiety by counting the number of bodies packed onto the dance floor, but I lost track almost before even getting started. There must have been nearly a thousand people crammed into the venue that night, sandwiched like sardines. I managed to maintain my composure, but I was internally cursing my friends for having left out critical details and plotting an early escape.

I ordered another drink from a friendly bartender who chuckled more than once at my French. I would fumble through a rough translation I found online while he listened patiently and tried to contain his amusement. He insisted on responding in English, which frustrated me at first, but I became grateful as I grew more intoxicated throughout the night. My friends disappeared into the crowd at some point. I took a sip and left the safety of the row of bars, nudging and weaving through the throngs of people. Near an inconspicuous corner, a narrow, dark hallway led to a creaky set of ascending stairs. Scantily clad groups trickled up and down the steps, piquing my curiosity. I took the stairs one by one, gripping the rail to my right to avoid losing my footing in the dark. The bass from the club below reverberated through the thin metal under my feet, threatening to pitch me off balance. At the top, the stairs emptied onto a covered terrace. There were no lights, but moonlight peeked from behind a neighboring building, bathing the terrace in a strange, otherworldly glow. Groups of people clumped together, whispering amid plumes of smoke. Smoking is a common social practice in France, and anyone spotted outside a club without a cigarette is met with suspicion. I scanned the deck for an open spot to duck out of view and sat down along the railing overlooking the street below. It was much calmer up here, the thud of trance music low and distant beneath me. From my left, I could feel someone watching me intensely. It seemed I hadn't found a place where I could avoid the curious gaze of French partygoers, at least not fast enough. I turned my head slowly. The boy from Paris.

He was pretty, with a vibrant youthfulness and a messy mop of brown hair. A plain black T-shirt hung loosely from his thin frame, his biceps peering out from the sleeves. His eyes were dark and brooding, his smile mischievous. He excused himself from a group of friends, snuffed his cigarette, and slid closer to me along the wall. He rattled off something in French, to which I giggled nervously and shook my head.

"Oh, you are American?" he said with a smirk.

"Yes, and my French is fucking awful," I replied.

He waved off my embarrassment and laughed, promising to practice his English with me. He was mesmerizing, his energy intoxicating. We talked for a bit, but I was so distracted by how much I wanted to kiss him that I can't remember a thing we said. Time seemed to stand still and move at lightning speed all at once. After a while, he leaned forward and put his lips on mine. The electricity of his touch shot from my lips all the way down my spine. His skin was softer than I expected, and he smelled faintly of cologne. He pulled back, stared me up and down, and offered his hand.

"Do you want to dance?" he asked gleefully.

We were attached for the rest of the night. His arm slipped instinctively around my neck, wrapping me in a gentle embrace as we whirled underneath the lights. From time to time, he would scan my eyes for the real, unpolished me beneath the carefully crafted exterior. Everything about him was tender and kind, as if untainted by the cruelty of the world outside. I wondered what he'd seen, what he'd been through. I pulled his hips closer, swaying in tandem to a deep electronic beat, and nuzzled my nose into his shoulder. It felt good to be held.

Michael and I spent most of my remaining days jetting from one corner of the city to the other. He would light up gleefully when we stumbled across a familiar landmark. A museum he had visited in grade school. A church his mother took him to on holidays. An old restaurant, packed full during lunchtime, where he used to sit and watch passersby on the street. We waited in a long line at the steps of Notre-Dame, its towering architecture casting long shadows on the cobblestones. It struck me that he was just as in awe as I was. Despite living in the city his entire life, its magnificence still rendered him speechless. He wasn't too busy to admire the beauty of its sights and people or allow its grandeur to be dimmed by a singular focus on the next hurdle to clear or dollar to make. He just reveled in it all, allowing its brilliance to wash over him. I was astounded by his almost childlike ability to find delight in it all. The curly-haired, baby-faced boy from Paris was hopelessly, inescapably in love with being alive.

The plane ride home felt days longer than the flight out. Rain had drizzled the window on the tarmac, leaving droplets streaking backward as we took off. I nibbled on pretzels and watched movies to distract myself, but I couldn't stop thinking about Paris. The crowded lunch tables in the afternoon, like the entire city stopped at midday to exhale in unity. The woman in her floral-print dress, a gleeful bounce in her step as she tidied the sidewalk in front of her. The boy named Michael watching me fade into the distance from the back seat of a taxi. These memories, created miles from home, seemed more luminous than others, their colors richer, their smells sharper. I didn't just remember the way the strobe lights gleamed on Michael's face the first night we danced; I remembered how that made me feel. It was as if just a bit of my numbness had thawed, its dull void replaced by the faintest energetic tingle. For the first time in a long time, I didn't just hear the world or see it—I felt it. I felt an exhilarating, intoxicating taste of the old me.

I didn't want to go back to living in shame for waking up each day. I no longer wanted to suffocate myself with misery out of fear. I sat back in the plush seat and smirked. I had waited with bated breath for someone to give me permission to live again, and I finally realized that only I had stood in the way.

Permission granted.

I've never been one to put much stock in the meanings of dreams. I know there's an entire market for people hoping to find hidden dream interpretations, but I've always considered myself a very pragmatic person. I like rational explanations, the kind we can understand through science and data. I find it far more believable that a particularly vivid dream is the result of a bad meatball rather than some commune with a different dimension. But from time to time, logic gives way to the inexplicable. Sometimes a dream seems to transcend what is knowable, leaving me to shrug and wonder, *What if?*

In the fall of 2019, I traveled to New York City to shoot an episode of the *TODAY* show. New York is a magnificent metropolis, full of life and seemingly boundless energy. People hustle to and from their responsibilities, jostling one another on the subway platform before rushing off to their next stop. They honk their horns incessantly, hopelessly stranded in predictable traffic but in a hurry to go nowhere nonetheless. I have always been fascinated by the sheer volume of people moving in harmony, like some intricate ballet choreographed to perfection by the universe itself. It is truly a wonder—so many lives and stories converging in a single place, woven together into a beautiful tapestry. It inspires awe and utterly overwhelms all at once.

I touched down in the early afternoon, a few hours before the end of the workday. It was already chilly outside, and a cold wind whistled between the buildings. I pulled the lapels of my overcoat tighter. I had a lot on my plate that day. Work was moving at a frenetic pace, I had more things on my to-do list than I knew what to do with, and the stress of preparing for the next day's interview hung above it all. I needed to get to my hotel before my daunting agenda escalated into full-blown panic.

I caught an Uber into the city and wriggled anxiously in the back seat. We sat behind a stream of brake lights on the highway. Orlando traffic is uniquely bad for a metro area of its size, but there is nothing quite as soul crushing as staring at your tiny, stationary car on a virtual map in New York. After a long crawl along highways and side streets, we pulled up to a boutique hotel just down the street from 30 Rockefeller Plaza. I wrapped my scarf tightly around my neck and lugged my suitcase through the front door.

The hotel was modern on the inside. A row of benches sat facing the narrow check-in desk. With her fingers clacking furiously against the keyboard of her computer, the well-dressed woman behind the counter told me that my room wasn't quite ready yet. I checked my suitcase with the bellhop and asked the front-desk agent to jot down a recommendation for a nearby coffee shop. It's far easier for me to get work done in the quiet of a private space, but I figured I'd make do while they finished putting a fresh pair of sheets on the bed. Holding the agent's recommendation in hand, I stepped out of the sliding doors of the hotel and into the cold city air.

I was blasted almost immediately by the wind. People often scoff at me for being sensitive to low temperatures. After all, I'm from Portland, a city full of people who celebrate cloudless, fifty-degree days with bikinis and sunbathing in the park. But I want to take this opportunity to set the record straight: what was cold then is still cold now. Maybe I was destined to be a Floridian because I spent all of my childhood with chattering teeth and sniffles. I have also spent most of my life perpetually underdressed for the weather. I wrapped my arms tightly around my chest and squeezed, hoping to generate enough body heat for the few blocks to the coffee shop. I stepped out from underneath the awning and was immediately knocked in the shoulder by a swift passerby. I tried to apologize, but she'd already jammed her open hand in my direction, shouting at me to get out of her way, her feet never skipping a beat. I stumbled back, steadying myself against the wall behind me, and adjusted the straps on my backpack. *Stay out of the way. Got it.*

I weaved my way down the sidewalk, sidewinding through the crowd. Halfway down the block, I decided it was too cold to continue, ducked inside a Mexican restaurant, and slid onto a bench by the window. The smell of freshly baked tortillas and chopped cilantro prompted my shoulders to lower and my heart to stop racing. I exhaled for what felt like the first time since bounding from the jet bridge and into my rideshare. I unzipped my backpack, then took out my laptop and placed it on the counter in front of me. I opened the computer and clicked the power button. Nothing. Dead. I let out an exasperated sigh and opened the bag again to search for my charger. Nothing. It was still in my suitcase back at the hotel.

Just as I was slipping my laptop back into my backpack and mentally preparing myself for the chilly walk back, I was bumped again. This time, the impatient culprit carried two large plastic cups full of soda fresh from the fountain. The lid popped free from one, and the contents exploded across my back, dripping down my neck onto the seat underneath me. The boy holding the cups blushed sheepishly, whirled on his heels, and disappeared into the crowd inside the restaurant. I couldn't hold back my tears. Dripping wet, cold, and falling further behind on work by the minute, I sat in the busy restaurant and cried. Everything about the trip had been overwhelming, and all I wanted to do was get on a plane, go back home, and crawl under the blankets I had emerged from earlier that morning.

The rest of the day wasn't much of an improvement. I got back to the hotel, picked up a pair of key cards from the front desk, and went upstairs to set up shop. The accommodations were cramped. I relegated the bursting suitcase to a dusty corner, wedging it between an old armoire and the wall underneath the window. A light breeze whistled through a crack in the window's seal. The desk was shallow and poorly lit, the light just barely bright enough to make out the words on a page through a squint. I positioned my computer on one end, the corner dangling precariously, and my notebook on the other. Each time I pressed my pen to the page, the notebook would tip over the edge toward the trash can. Irked, I pushed back from the wooden table and retired to the bed. I crawled under the thin sheet and laid my head down on a pillow that wasn't very soft. I'm typically a very light sleeper, finding it difficult to doze off without first getting perfectly comfortable, but the weight of the day hung heavy on my shoulders, and I soon drifted off to sleep.

I'm probably going into painstaking detail because I'm still trying to rationalize the dream I had that night. I had been under enormous pressure all day. I was falling behind on important work and facing a high-profile interview that made me nervous. Everything that could have gone wrong seemed to have gone wrong. New York City had worn my nerves down to frayed stems. Maybe the dream reflected those stressors, an anxiety made inevitable by the chaos of the prior twelve hours. Maybe it was a physical manifestation of the pumpkin ice cream I had decided to eat just before falling asleep. Or maybe it really did mean something more: a timely message from somewhere beyond human comprehension, designed to shake me and put it all back in focus.

I had barely dozed off when I was jolted awake again, this time in the back seat of a speeding car. Outside the window, trees whizzed by, barely more than a fuzzy green blur. The seat beneath me was covered in a soft gray fabric. I rubbed it with one hand, reveling in how good it felt against my skin. I didn't recognize the driver, and I'm confident to this day that I had never seen him before. He wore funny fingerless leather gloves, the hair on his knuckles dark and bushy. He glanced into the rearview mirror more than once, as if to confirm that I was still there. The car flew over deep potholes, jostling and jouncing me around. I tugged on the seat belt to make sure it was fastened. It was all so vivid—*too* vivid. I knew right away that I was dreaming because the colors were just a touch too vibrant. The green of the leaves was brighter than usual, their hue so electric that I had to squint to keep from wincing. The roar of the engine was sharp, as if its gears and pistons were bouncing haphazardly in my lap. The texture of the seat was so intense that it sent tingles running through my fingers and up my arms. Everything around me seemed to glow, like each object was framed by a radiant halo.

When my eyes had finally adjusted to the intensity of my surroundings, I realized that I wasn't alone in the back seat. Next to me, I could make out two distinct pairs of skinny legs, one pressed into a pair of tight jeans and the other jutting from the ragged edges of cutoffs. I turned my head slowly, aware that the warmth of this vivid dream might abruptly morph into the cold horror of a nightmare, depending on who was sitting next to me. I gazed, dumbfounded, into the two familiar faces smiling back at me: Drew and Juan.

They appeared simultaneously just as I remembered them and strangely different. Their auras were brighter; they were somehow younger and more refreshed. The same pleasant glow that surrounded everything else was even more pronounced around them, a golden shimmer dancing about their heads. They seemed happy, but not in the way one appears after getting a long-awaited Christmas gift or enjoying a favorite dessert. Drew and Juan looked as if every burden had lifted from them, their bodies suspended in the weightlessness of existence without pain. Drew grinned as the shock washed over me, his cheek scrunching up on one side in typical fashion. We sat there gazing at each other for a few breathless seconds, neither of us daring to disrupt the silence. I held back my words, afraid that the slightest sound would shatter the fragile vision. Juan finally giggled, unable to contain his excitement.

I wanted to say so many things. I wanted to tell them how hard I had been fighting for the world to remember them. I wanted to catch them up on all the inside jokes I wished they could be part of. I wanted to brag about my successes at work and complain about my latest failed first date. There was so much joy in sitting next to them again, as if no time had passed at all. But there was still a deep, nagging sadness at my core. There they sat, beside me, as vivid as they had been in life. But they also felt distant, fleeting, separated by an invisible force tugging us apart with each passing second. I somehow understood that our time together was limited, so I stammered the first words I could think of. "I miss you so much."

Drew giggled. "We miss you too. But we're so proud of you."

I couldn't hold in my emotions anymore. Tears burst from within, my sobs rattling my shoulders. "I am so sorry," I began. "I am so sorry I did this to you. I wish I could go back and fix it all. I wish I could tell you to ignore my messages. I wish I could give you back to your parents. I wish you could see how much we all need you." I paused, choking back my uncontrollable cries. "I wish you could come home."

Drew reached out and put his hand on my arm to quiet me. His expression was as warm as before, his energy unchanged by the trembling in my voice. "No more sadness," he said. "You can't hold on to this anymore. You have to let it—let us—go. We love you more than you will ever know."

I grabbed his hand, feeling its soft warmth. He was right. Every minute I spent under the thumb of my self-imposed guilt, fueled by my toxic need to earn each day on earth, pushed me further and further from memories like these. I had wasted countless hours worrying about whether I was responsible for what happened, time that I should have spent living the kind of bountiful life that Drew and Juan deserved to be living. I needed to let go of the helpless, tortured vision I had created of my best friends. Not so that I could forget them but so that I could remember them as they truly were. I didn't need to prevent myself from living as an act of penance. I needed to live—to *choose* to live—more fully, in honor of what they left behind. I wiped my cheek and glanced up to thank Drew.

His expression had darkened a bit, tinged by sadness. "We have to go now," he whispered.

"Please don't," I said frantically, tears welling up again. "There's so much more I want to tell you."

"There's no time now," he replied. "I don't know when we'll see you again. But know this: you were meant for this. It's time to release yourself from all you've been carrying and go live the life you were destined for. We will always love you."

I opened my mouth to speak, desperate to hold on to them for as long as possible, but no sound came out. A tightness in my throat rendered me silent as the vibrant contrasts of that dream world began to fade. A warm light enveloped everything, engulfing the unfamiliar driver and bathing the emerald trees in a wash of gold. Just before my friends dissolved into the light, Drew grinned one last time. *You got this,* he seemed to say.

CHAPTER 10

SAFE SPACE

When I say that community saved my life more than once, I mean it literally. After the shooting, there were many points at which I wondered whether being alive was worth it anymore. The darkest thoughts always lurked, but they were loudest when I was alone. Curled up in a ball under my blanket, I quietly wondered if falling asleep and never waking up would be so bad. Sitting on the couch next to a half-empty bottle of Scotch, I silently imagined my own lifeless body on the hardwood. At my lowest, I couldn't convince myself that anyone would notice if I were gone. But one by one, resolved to see the spark return to my eyes, the people around me nudged me back from the edge.

The woman who knelt with me in the grass after that first candlelight vigil was just being kind. She didn't filter her level of care through assumptions about my political beliefs or religious affiliation. Her compassion wasn't conditional. As it did for so many others in the community, the most gut-wrenching of tragedies engendered an innately human response: to care for and nurture those in pain. I'm heartbroken when I see who we've become, fighting our natural inclination to feel empathy and exercise compassion. I see people giving in to our ugliest impulses—the fear of losing control, the mistrust of things we don't understand. I watch as polarized plotlines and tweet-size sound bites tear us apart at the seams, which only works to enrich those who have more than they know what to do with. There is no hope for humanity if we are intent on going it alone. We didn't claw our way up the food chain by forging a million individual, unrelated paths. We built communities. We worked together. At our best, we've acknowledged that our collective advancement is only possible if we see the value in others. Unprompted, the woman in the grass saw mine. She took time to invest in me, not because there was a reward waiting but because, at her core, she knew I needed her. And in doing so, she saved my life.

Drew was happiest when he was bringing others together. I didn't fully understand it for most of our friendship. He was always reminding me to "fix my face" and be friendlier to others at the bar. He would prod me to introduce myself to the boy I had been eyeing from across the room. And if he planned a party with his diverse set of friends, you'd better have a solid excuse for not being able to attend. It took me too many years to piece it all together, but he was collecting us—his friends, his chosen family. And once he'd collected us, he protected us. He sought to save our lives, every day, reminding us that we were appreciated and loved, daring us to see the inherent value in ourselves. The magic of that refuge—the refuge Drew created for all of us—wasn't in my favorite leather chair next to the shelf that held all of our favorite movies. It wasn't in our usual purlieu on the patio of Pulse, with a perfect view of the stars overhead. It wasn't in the back seat of his Volkswagen Jetta, where I set up a fort of pillows and blankets and binged movies on my iPad while he sped us to our next New Year's Eve destination. The refuge was our little community. Drew's island of misfit toys, each with its own special spot and its own role to play. We were the sanctuary, the lifeline for others like us. He was teaching us how to build the shelter for ourselves.

In the wake of the shooting, a few of us launched The Dru Project, an organization that borrowed its name from Drew's social media handles. Our goal was nebulous at first: *Keep the best parts of him alive.* We weren't initially sure what that meant. But as we huddled around a bottle of Drew's favorite wine and started sketching out what that *could* mean, the mission took shape hastily. Drew was best known for his innate ability to create spaces that included everyone. He had proudly launched a Gay–Straight Alliance club in high school, despite living in a part of the country that worships Confederate flags and billboards with half-naked women carrying machine guns. He didn't care that his efforts might stoke the bigots roaming the aisles of the local grocery store. He wanted to provide a haven for kids like himself, a place for them to be who they were without fear. He wanted to *be* a safe space.

Halfway through that bottle of wine, we had our epiphany. Just as Drew had been a safe space for others while he was alive, he could still create safe spaces now that he was gone. The idea came with a personal revelation for me too. I had spent decades searching for a safety I wasn't sure I deserved. I hunted for it in late-night rendezvous, new homes, nightclubs. But the only thing that had ever really made me feel safe was my chosen family. It was Drew. Now I was tasked with helping others find that shelter from the tempest around them *before* they packed suitcases and went in search of it halfway across the world. My safe space had been stolen. Shattered. Ripped away. But in an instant, I came to terms with the understanding that I would never get it back. And that maybe helping others find their safe spaces could be good enough.

~

I pulled up to the curb outside the memorial site and set the parking brake. It was the summer of 2019, more than three years after the shooting. But the night air still hung as heavy as the night that everything changed. The neighborhood was dark and still, the only lights those from the building itself, pouring onto the concrete below. I stepped out of the car and sidled up to the fence outside, adorned with pictures, rainbow flags, and colorful mementos. In the late hours of the day, long after the sun had set and curious visitors had returned to their hotels, a quiet sense of peace floated above the space. I prefer being there at night. The solitude is a relief. The rush of traffic has dissipated. Curious passersby have all gone home. It's reverent. I feel closer to the boys that way.

I walked the perimeter of the fence, running my fingers along faded birthday cards and wilted flower petals. Each one of the countless tributes reflected a grieving heart. A mother mourning the loss of her child. A sibling yearning for the sound of his brother's voice. A friend still crying out for the one who stole a piece of his heart. Collectively, they represent our greatest pain. Whole neighborhoods with pieces carved out. Entire groups of people desperate for the monotony of life before Pulse, before a city was scarred by bullet holes and forty-nine people died. All of it silently captured in bits of paper fluttering in a gentle night breeze. I stopped and knelt by a picture of Drew and Juan, their arms over one another's shoulders, their shirts still crisp and vibrant.

"God, we miss you," I whispered, glancing around to ensure that no one overheard me.

A frog trilled in a nearby bush, the only other sound piercing the peaceful silence. In the quiet, I could almost hear them whispering back to me. Reminding me to live a little. Daring me to let go of the grudges and pain that I insisted on lugging around. Challenging me not to lose sight of the community that binds us all together. It's as if they can tell when the work hits a snag or we wander too far from our purpose. Their voices rustle with the leaves overhead, murmuring a gentle reminder that if we are truly committed to a future fit for everyone, our only path is forward.

I glanced back at the picture, its details unchanged. I wondered if they'd had any inkling of the kind of impact they had on others, the sense of belonging they bestowed on so many.

At a young age, I packed two suitcases and took a leap of faith to find somewhere I belonged. Up to that point, I had known only a world where being all of me was a liability, where survival was only guaranteed by shutting up and blending in, living within the bounds of the box created for me. But I believed that there had to be something better, somewhere I could be celebrated rather than controlled. I was in desperate need of a place—a building, a neighborhood, a city—where I could live outside the lines and dare to be more than the script assigned to me. In the end, I found it. Somewhere to matter. A chosen family to adopt. A community to call home. The amorphous thing I was searching for wasn't tucked away in the dark corner of a bar or under the dazzling lights of a disco ball. Because physical spaces are temporary, fleeting structures that age and decay. A parking lot is repaved and transformed into a memorial. A club is shuttered and boarded up, the stench of death too strong to wash away. But the community remains, untethered to a single spot on a map and unchained to a single point in time.

I grazed the faded image one more time and smiled.

For a world you'd be proud of.

AFTERWORD

The best advice I got before embarking on this journey was from my friend Joy Reid. She was among the first people I called when I decided to take the plunge and write a memoir, and among the first to earnestly encourage me to put my journey to paper. She's an accomplished author, compelling storyteller, and powerful media presence, and when she speaks, people listen. So naturally, I couldn't wait to get her thoughts on my decision to begin the process of writing a book. I sent her a text one afternoon to share the good news and pick her brain. Joy's advice came back almost instantly: Take time to write. She explained that making time didn't mean carving out an hour after a long workday or getting up early on a weekend to stare at the blinking cursor on my laptop screen. She urged me to clear my calendar, leave work behind, and create meaningful space to relive some of the most challenging periods of my life and weave them together with purpose.

"Six weeks is ideal," she said.

For a type A personality grappling with a nasty case of workaholism and living in a culture that values productivity over all else, the idea of taking six weeks off to marinate in my own thoughts was petrifying. Who would do my work while I was gone? What the hell does unplugging mean in today's social media rat race? What if I couldn't figure out where to start? What would I do in the dark recesses of my mind for an extended period of time—alone? I had all but decided to ignore Joy's sage advice and try writing in the tiny crevices of free time

I could carve out of life, but then my boss echoed Joy's sentiments. She called one morning to inform me that the entire office team planned to pool its resources to cover my duties and give me the space I needed. It takes an incredible amount of privilege to be able to say that, and I don't know if I'll ever find sufficient words to thank my peers for their support. But with so many people urging me to prioritize this journey and willingly investing in my success, I was left with no other choice. I relented and planned my time away. I settled on four weeks and finagled my schedule to work a few longer days and lighten the load for others while I was gone.

I was sure of one thing from the jump: sitting in my tiny apartment for four weeks would result in a boatload of nothing. Let's be honest, seven hundred square feet of living space isn't conducive to creating. The wobbly stool I bought online and put together after a few glasses of rosé barely fits under my desk, and there are ample distractions at home: laundry that needs doing, a run to the mailbox that just can't wait, that thing from Target I've been meaning to pick up. Staying home would give me every excuse to avoid writing anything. Writing through the messy details of one's life requires emotional labor, and sitting in the familiar environs of my apartment would give me all the tools necessary to avoid it. I needed to uproot myself, change my setting entirely. As Joy had said, I needed meaningful space to reflect.

I wasn't sure what kind of inspirations (or distractions) I would find in Puerto Vallarta, but I knew that it had served me as a place to recharge in the past. The lush green jungle. The crystal-blue Pacific waters crashing against the sand. Handsome boys with sun-kissed skin and carefree laughs. Vibrant colors, mouthwatering flavors, and a limitless supply of tequila. It's a beachside paradise that I've used as an escape from the grueling pace of work before—the perfect place to burrow away, melt into a state of anonymity, and get intimate with my own creative process. Before I could talk myself out of it, I booked a flight and a little apartment just a few blocks from the water.

The day had already been a long one, and I had no intent of stopping on the walk home. Despite warnings from virtually everyone I know, I regularly forget to apply sunscreen. After I had spent many hours stretched out on the sand, my shoulders were tinged with a reddish hue and sensitive to the touch. I needed to get home and lie down. I was feeling bolstered, though, having hit my word-count goal for the third day in a row, so I decided to take an unplanned detour by the pier. The sun would set in less than an hour, and Mother Nature was already painting the sky with brilliant reds and oranges. The pier sits just a few yards off the coast, with a twisted spire reaching up toward the clouds. A ring of benches surrounds its base, inviting visitors to plop down and let the sounds of the ocean wash over them. I stopped to take a few photos, marveling at the canvas of colors dancing above the water. After I'd captured a few dozen shots, I turned and headed up the concrete stairs toward the street. A few vendors peddled wares along the sidewalk as I meandered up the hill to a familiar intersection. Just across the cobblestones, I caught a glimpse of a server carrying a pizza to the patio of one of my favorite local spots. My stomach growled approvingly. *All right,* I thought, *a quick bite to eat.*

I never could have imagined that a slice of pepperoni pizza and a mango mojito would walk me right into a defining crossroads in this process. Sitting in a corner near the window was a woman named Elena. She was unassuming at first glance. Diminutive in stature. A breezy blouse hung from her shoulders, and tan skin peeked out from underneath. I almost didn't notice her, tucked back against a window. But before I had even crawled up onto my stool, I could feel her energy radiating throughout the cramped café. Her hair was untamed, teased by the salty ocean air. Her voice carried through the restaurant, its trills inviting more than one guest to stop and say hello. With a gleam that seemed born of impulse and breathtaking adventure, her weathered face silently told the story of an entire life's journey. She gestured grandly toward my space at the bar and welcomed me with an enchanting timbre to her voice.

"Come on in," she said with disarming warmth.

We exchanged customary pleasantries. Chatted about being Americans abroad. Complained about failed COVID-19 responses. Raved about Mexican delicacies like mescal and aguachile. I am naturally an introverted person, so I normally do everything in my power to dodge idle conversation with strangers. But after a few minutes, and more than a few sips of our drinks, our exchange took a more personal turn. We talked about home: how desperately we wished Americans could slow down to enjoy life, like those who live here. We talked about the escapism that travel provides. Elena asked what brought me to Mexico this time around. I gulped instinctively. Writing a memoir is an inherently vulnerable act. You invite the world into some of the deepest, darkest parts of who you are, and you dare them to try to make better sense of it than you can. But if I've learned anything during this journey, it's that vulnerability is the purpose. Humanity needs us to be more vulnerable and courageous. It begs us to be real with one another if we're ever going to get through this as a species. I swallowed my ego and cleared my throat.

"I'm writing my first book . . . a memoir," I stammered, my lips locked on to my mojito.

Elena's head cocked to one side, silently inviting me to go on. As I detailed the themes of the book—struggling at the intersections of identity, finding safety in community, discovering purpose in the wake of tragedy—her gaze was steady. Occasionally, her brow furrowed skeptically. But she listened intently. I got through my elevator pitch, and my voice trailed off. Elena's lips pursed. Then she asked me the question that upended my writing retreat: *Why does it matter?* I'm sure that the restaurant was as loud and raucous as ever, but a deafening pregnant pause followed. How do you respond to that? I had just laid bare my vulnerable self to a stranger, and she basically replied with a shrug.

"Maybe your life is remarkable," she continued. "Maybe it isn't. But we all have trauma. Every single one of us. Why will sharing yours make mine any easier to deal with? How will picking your book up off the shelf make a difference in my life?"

I froze. I'd considered the question of this book's purpose before, spent countless hours grappling with impostor syndrome as a first-time author, and lived for years with a persistent dread that sharing my story is just a selfish act of ego wrapped in flowery language and a well-tailored suit. But I had never been confronted so directly with that hard truth: *We all have trauma.* We all struggle. Why does mine matter? I'm a firm believer that it's a fruitless endeavor to try to compare the hurdles that each of us is tasked with overcoming. So where do I get the audacity to write about mine?

I don't have the answers, but that's the point. No one has written a foolproof road map for how to get through life's pitfalls. No one is the ultimate authority on struggle, pain, or the right way to heal. We all hold different pieces of the puzzle. A revelation in a therapy session here. A lesson learned in the throes of crisis there. Heartbreak and grief in between. Sharing our painful learning is not about proclaiming expertise but about vulnerably flashing a few of the scars that make us human, and inviting others to do the same.

We—all of us—have been through hell. The globe is engulfed in turmoil. A pandemic has ravaged our communities, cries for racial justice continue to go unanswered, and cultural fractures threaten to rip democracy to shreds. I hear whispers of exhaustion and fatigue from the strongest people I know, signs of an unsustainable struggle to carry the weight of the world on their individual shoulders. The truth is, the most important lesson I learned after Pulse also seems to be the timeliest: we can only get through these trying times together. The intense grief and suffering we have experienced in just the past few years are nearly unfathomable. We've had a collective front-row seat to mass death. We have known pain on an unimaginable scale. We have seen blunders and mismanagement that put our friends and families in caskets. It's impossible to ignore how much trauma and struggle each of us has been through.

This book merely attempts to ask the logical question: Now what? What do we do with the unresolved agony of losing so many people we loved? How do we stitch together a society severed by incendiary rhetoric and callous political opportunism? At a time when it's tempting to see our neighbors as *others* rather than as people like us, how do we even begin to care for ourselves and our communities?

As I said, I'm not the expert. None of us is. I'm not here to prescribe the path forward for anyone. If someone tells you they have all the answers, run in the opposite direction as expeditiously as possible. I'm simply inviting you on my own journey. Joy. Pain. Love. Loss. I wanted to create a quiet space for us to be honest and authentic with each other, if only for a brief while, in these pages. I wanted to assure you that exploring and contending with the dark crevices of your own emotions is not weakness—it is courage. And for Elena, I wanted to answer that our stories matter because when we share them, the collective pieces of our individual lived experiences teach us all how to go on.

I am not so arrogant as to believe that my life is any more remarkable than anyone else's. I just wanted to tell you what I've learned about finding light in the darkest of hours, to remind you that with our backs against the wall, we find a way out together. I am daring us to marshal the power in our collective struggle to find healing and hope. I'm grateful that you took the plunge with me.

ACKNOWLEDGMENTS

So much goes into three decades of life. So many paths crossed and decision points traversed. For that reason, there are truly an infinite number of people who deserve thanks for helping me get this far—and for helping me find the courage to share what I've learned along the way. But in the interest of keeping the end of this book brief, I'll name just a few.

Thank you, in advance, to my family. For understanding the importance of this journey for me. For being endlessly proud of me, even for what feels like the smallest of achievements. And for being willing to grow alongside me.

Thank you to Sara and Shawn, the pair of friends who have kept me afloat for the past six years. Thank you for being willing to read my drafts at their roughest and letting me vent when it seemed the wheels might be coming off.

Thank you to Sally Hogshead for daring me to dream bigger and reach higher. Thank you for making the right introductions so that this project could take flight. Your boundless energy and optimism are qualities that have often given me a necessary nudge to finish what I started.

Thank you to Nadine Smith, a mentor and world-class leader, for pushing me to lean in to my vulnerability. Men are taught from a young age that to be vulnerable is to be weak, that to explore emotion is to abandon masculinity. In our time together, you have always sought to shatter those misconceptions. You will never fully know the profound impact your tutelage has had on me—or how it shaped this book.

Thank you to Selena James and Jason Kirk, the sculptors who took the disheveled lump of clay that was my collection of ideas and molded it into something to be proud of. Jason, your ability to weave praise into careful attention to detail set the words in my mind free. And, Selena, you believed in me from the start. I will forever be grateful that I could place my first work in your care.

Thank you to Jud Laghi, the literary agent who took my call and turned it into this incredible adventure. Thank you for not only believing in my story but for taking such care to help craft it. You have gone above and beyond, ready at a moment's notice to give advice, shape a paragraph, or hammer out the final title. Thank you for seeing the ways in which the tale of a young, queer, Black kid might resonate with people around the globe.

Thank you to my late mother for giving me my strength of character. For reading books to me before bed, sparking my curiosity for reading. For teaching me to always keep my chin up. I hope every day that I am making you proud.

And finally, thank you to Drew and Juan. For introducing me to myself. For never doubting what I was capable of. For challenging me to live with conviction. For pushing me outside my shell. For being the protagonists in my story. For loving me without condition.

ABOUT THE AUTHOR

Photo © 2022 Sean Black

Brandon J. Wolf is a survivor of the 2016 terror attack at Pulse nightclub in Orlando and a nationally recognized public speaker and advocate for LGBTQ+ civil rights and gun-safety reform. Wolf has written opinion pieces for CNN.com, Oprah Daily, *USA Today, Newsweek,* and *Out* magazine. In 2019, he became the first survivor of the tragedy at Pulse to testify before Congress. Wolf has since delivered keynote addresses at the 2022 Netroots Nation conference, NYC Pride, Ohio State University, Penn State University, Florida State University, Howard Brown, and more. He joined Senator Elizabeth Warren's presidential campaign in 2019 and became a top national surrogate, doing tours in Iowa, South Carolina, Michigan, Nevada, and Florida. Wolf is a frequent contributor on MSNBC's *The ReidOut* and *American Voices with Alicia Menendez* and serves as the press secretary for Equality Florida. For more information, visit www.brandonwolf.us.